∾

Spiritual Excellence

Alban Goodier, S.J.

Spiritual Excellence

How to Make Progress
in Prayer and Love

SOPHIA INSTITUTE PRESS®
Manchester, New Hampshire

Spiritual Excellence: How to Make Progress in Prayer and Love is an abridged edition of *The School of Love and Other Essays* (St. Meinrad, Indiana: Grail Publications, 1947). This 2002 edition by Sophia Institute Press® includes minor editorial revisions to the original text and an appendix of prayers.

Sophia Institute Press®
Box 5284, Manchester, NH 03108
1-800-888-9344
www.sophiainstitute.com

Nihil obstat: Innocent Apap, O.P., *Censor deputatus*
Imprimatur: Edm. Can. Surmont, *Vicarius Generalis*
Westminster, December 14, 1919

Library of Congress Cataloging-in-Publication Data

Goodier, Alban, 1869-1939.
    [School of love and other essays]
    Spiritual excellence : how to make progress in prayer and
      love / Alban Goodier.
      p. cm.
    Originally published: The school of love and other essays.
      St. Meinrad, Ind. : Grail Publications, 1947.
    ISBN 1-928832-69-5 (pbk. : alk. paper)
    1. Spiritual life — Catholic Church. I. Title.
    BX2350.3 .G665 2002
    248.4'82 — dc21   2002010255

02 03 04 05 06 07 08 09 10 9 8 7 6 5 4 3 2 1

~

Contents

∽

∾

Spiritual Excellence

Editor's note: The biblical quotations in the following pages are taken from the Douay-Rheims edition of the Old and New Testaments. Where applicable, quotations have been cross-referenced with the differing names and enumeration in the Revised Standard Version, using the following symbol: (RSV =).

Chapter One

Determine whether your love is true

"Be zealous for the better gifts," says St. Paul. "And I show unto you yet a more excellent way."[1] Then the apostle breaks out into that wonderful description of love which has been worn threadbare by all writers and preachers; worn threadbare, and yet it is ever new, ever thrilling, ever inspiring. "Love is patient, is kind. Love envieth not, dealeth not perversely; is not puffed up, is not ambitious, seeketh not her own, is not provoked to anger, thinketh no evil, rejoiceth not in iniquity, but rejoiceth with the truth; beareth all things, believeth all things, hopeth all things, endureth all things. Love never falleth away. . . . Follow after love."[2]

Love is a word we play with very easily. We use it for the most trifling emotions. We even use it with a sense

[1] 1 Cor. 12:31.
[2] 1 Cor. 13:4-8; 14:1.

of evil, so that we almost fear to have it on our lips at all, lest others take scandal at our language. Nevertheless, the word is the greatest and the deepest that the human tongue has ever invented. It is almost too deep for definition. Poets have extolled it from the beginning of the world. Philosophers have discussed and analyzed it. Men and women have lived for it and died for it by millions. Upon it man builds up this existence and God Himself has built eternity. It is the key to this life, the content of the next, the abiding link between both, the mortal's possession that can never die, the fire of life that leaps across the chasm made by death.

Love, then, almost laughs at definition. It is too vivid, too burning a thing to be defined. If it could be adequately defined — no doubt it can — it would still have no meaning for us; it would almost appear contemptible, unless we ourselves had known it by experience.

A man understands what love is, and has love in him, insofar as he has himself actually loved, and does love, and no further. Philosophy will not teach him the real thing; poetry will not help him much. When he has left it, and has been stirred by it, and has longed, at least, and striven to be something and to do something because of it, then, and to that extent, he will know it.

He will know, too, that he has not reached its end, that there are other depths of love that he has not attained. He may reach them someday; meanwhile it is something to have discovered what he knows.

Hence, for the understanding of love, it is more important to describe than to define it; to see it in its effects rather than on paper; to watch it in its growth and making, so that, if we really wish for it, we may follow the path that leads toward it. And the key to it is given to us in the very simple words of one who certainly knew.

"Love," says a certain great master of the science, "is seen in deeds rather than in words." That is the key to the whole matter: the deeds that love will make us do. Let us, then, watch love in action; above all, let us watch it as it beats against the bars of its prison within our own hearts. For it is there most of all, perhaps there only, that we can read it securely for ourselves, and according to the measure of our own capacity, without any fear of being misled, without any danger of getting out of our depth. "The kingdom of God," said our Lord, "is within you";[3] and the kingdom of God is nothing if not the kingdom of Love.

[3] Luke 17:21.

Spiritual Excellence

What, then, do I understand by a loving nature, the good ground on which the seed of love is likely to bear most abundant fruit? I understand, first of all, a nature that is easily led to think little of itself. It is a nature that, as it were, is easily distracted from itself by appreciation and admiration of that which it finds around it and in others. Outside itself it is forever discovering matter of interest, something worth attention, so that to itself it forgets to give much thought.

Such a trait is common in children, and we love them for it. To them, until they are spoiled, all the world is new and wonderful; themselves they have not yet discovered. We see it in great poets and great artists. Love of that which inspires them is their life; it makes them unlike other men, and the common human nature that is in us all makes us claim for them forgiveness for much excess because we know they have loved much.[4]

Second, by a loving nature I understand a nature of deep emotions. Not merely does it see and appreciate, but it is affected by its appreciations; it suffers in one way or another. There are some natures that fall short of

[4] Cf. Luke 7:36-47.

this. They can appreciate the beautiful, they can analyze it, they can describe it, in some sense they can be interested in it, but to be moved by it in any undue degree would seem to them a weakness. Such natures may attain much more, especially by way of intellect, but if emotion does not follow, their love is a crippled thing. Love feels joy; love feels sorrow. When it joys, its joy may swell until it becomes an agony and it is compelled to cry out, "No more, no more!" When it sorrows, its sorrow may be worse than death, and yet it will cherish it with a sense of nature satisfied. When it has neither joy nor sorrow, then, whatever else there may be, life is like an empty desert.

Third, by a loving nature I understand a nature that can act. True love demands a certain courage, a certain daring, to act, not merely by the dictate of reason, but also by the prompting of love. True, it is liable to make mistakes; it may be convicted of much foolishness, of many excesses of generosity. Love does not always calculate, does not always consider pros and cons, is not always prudent as some philosophers understand that virtue, does not always look for success, but once aroused, shuts its eyes, "gives and does not count the cost, fights and does not heed the wounds, toils and does not seek for rest, labors and looks for no reward,"[5] lays down its life and does not think about it. Such a nature is dangerous? Yes, but it is dangerous to go into battle; it is dangerous to go out upon the mission field; it is dangerous to tend the diseased; it is of the essence of all greatness to face what is dangerous. "Greater love than this no man hath, that he lay down his life for his beloved,"[6] whoever or whatever that beloved may be.

Such is a loving nature, as it comes from the hand of God. The development of that nature is the meaning of this life. It may be cultivated and fostered so that it may become capable of ever more. It may be clipped and dwarfed so that in the end it droops into a pitiable weed. It may be grown on artificial lines, pruned into a caricature of nature, so that it develops like those boxwood or yew-tree imitations of birds, or animals, or chairs, which in an artificial age were once thought to be beautiful.

And if it may be cultivated, obviously it will be along the three lines that have been already pointed out. If

---

[5] From a prayer of St. Ignatius of Loyola (1491-1556), founder of the Society of Jesus.

[6] Cf. John 15:13.

true love is disinterested, he who wishes to cultivate the power of loving will cultivate disinterestedness.

If true love is moved by strong emotion, the devotee of love will let himself be drawn by emotion as well as by reason, however much reason may hold the reins. He will not submit to be imprisoned in his own shallow argumentation and will not be narrowed down by his own blinking vision. He will overlap himself in his esteem of and longing for objects that are more precious than himself.

Lastly, and consequently, the man who wishes truly to love and to know to the full what love means, will beware of that timid, limping thing which sometimes parades, and hides its littleness, under the name of prudence. He will have a large horizon, reaching out beyond the range of life. He will learn the art of giving, with a hand outspread, as if all he had were but for this purpose. He will live with a large and unflinching generosity, reveling in the freedom from pettiness of whatever kind, "envying not, dealing not perversely, seeking not his own," but always "rejoicing with the truth." This is the atmosphere in which love grows.

In the same way, I may test and examine such degree of love as I possess; for little as it is, that it is none I will not allow. St. Teresa[7] once described Hell as "the place where there is no love"; and in spite of all its miseries, my soul has not yet come to that. Crawling and bleeding though it be from many wounds, there is yet life in it; and if life, then love.

But has that love grown straight or crooked? Is it growing straight or crooked now? Is it wholly true, or is it partly true and partly false? And if the latter, is the false so growing on the true that the flower is becoming blighted, the fruit rotting at the core, however fair it may seem without?

Let us see.

If what has been said is sound, the less my love has a thought for itself, so much truer it is. It seeks not its own; it is not for mere pleasure that it loves, nor for the pleasurable consequences, unless it be the joy of its nature fulfilled, the joy of giving and of sacrifice. Sweetness indeed may be there, and sweetness of such kind as alone deserves the name. But not on its account is love pursued. To pursue it for its sake is the throttling of love, making it a slave instead of a master, using it for some

---

[7] St. Teresa of Avila (1515-1582), Carmelite nun and mystic who reformed her order.

other end, when it is itself the noblest and only end of all. Is my love of this caliber?

Second, if my love does not stir me, or stirs me only a very little, less than many other motives that make their impression on me, it is tending to die. A stoic, ancient or modern, who boasts of being above emotion, who acts by his reason and that only, who prides himself on doing his duty, has triumphed over love — scotched it if he has not killed it. It is a gruesome triumph, the triumph of the polar ice over the underlying land. Beauty there may be of a kind, beauty and strength and stillness; but life and warmth and growth and fruitfulness there cannot be.

But love stirs all the strings upon the human heart. Sometimes, even, it sweeps its master-hand across them and stirs them all together so that the poor, dear, enviable human creature is all joy and all agony at once. Because they are not its own, because they are the joys and the sorrows of others, they are multiplied beyond control, each beating up against the other, sometimes in harmony, sometimes in discord, but always throbbing with a sympathy that others instinctively detect. At last the poor, loving heart does not know itself, does not know whether to call itself happy or distressed, tossed as it is upon the billows of emotion, torn by the cries, scorched by the tears of all the creatures it loves. It wonders at itself and its capacity for suffering and asks itself, trembling, whether it has chosen the right path after all, is consoled by nothing that others understand by consolation, and sees death as its only escape from the whirl and tangle of emotion.

To how many lives of loving saints is not this the key? Is it not the key to the Heart of Christ Himself, and to His agony in the garden? Is it the key to my heart?

Third, love is a restless thing. Idleness and love are incompatible; love cannot go to sleep. This does not necessarily mean activity in the sense that men usually understand. It need not be doing anything, but it means that it is ever awake and on fire within the depths of its own heart. What it can give it gives; it longs to give what it cannot. It bankrupts itself, and counts its bankruptcy as gain. It glories in so having nothing, for the very having nothing proves that it is master of all. "The kingdom of Heaven is likened to a treasure hidden in a field, which, a man having found, hid it, and for joy thereof goeth, and selleth all that he hath, and buyeth that field. Again, the kingdom of Heaven is like to a merchant seeking good pearls, who, when he had found one pearl of great price, went his way, and sold all that he had, and bought it."[8]

Of course, this does not mean that love leads inevitably to poverty. Sometimes it does; sometimes it demands a surrender even of the things of earth. A husband gives all to his wife, a wife to her husband. Many a man has beggared himself for love of a noble cause. Still, these are but the trappings of love, which may or may not be present. A millionaire can love as well as a pauper; where love leads, a pauper can give as much as a millionaire. For it is the gift of ourselves that matters — the gift of a human heart, its homage, its reverence, its service, the outpouring of itself, in whatever condition it may be placed, the giving of its life, whether that life is destined to live on or is demanded as a present sacrifice. "Christ loved me, and gave Himself for me,"[9] says St. Paul, dumbfounded at the holocaust; and he answers with an eloquence that will hardly find its match in literature: "I am sure that neither death, nor life, nor angels, nor principalities, nor powers, nor things present, nor things to come, nor might, nor height, nor depth,

[8] Matt. 13:44-46.
[9] Cf. Gal. 2:20.

nor any other creature shall be able to separate us from the love of God, which is in Christ Jesus, our Lord."[10]

So does true love impel. Love impels to love; love impelled to love has love for its reward; its beginning and its end is only love. Is my love of this nature? For this is the third and final test.

Yes, as we have already said that, when we look at love aright, we see that to love demands great courage. To love perfectly is the greatest heroism; even lesser heroism is what it is because of the love that inspires it. There is something terrible in love. It is exacting; it is almost merciless. It will have the whole or nothing. Above all, it will have no rapine in the holocaust; it will abide no giving with one hand and taking back with the other. If you wish to love well and deeply, you must be prepared to lose, to "lay down your life for your friend," and to lay down, if need be, everything that is of less moment than life. What, in matter of fact, you may be asked for, you do not know. It may be the laying down of life; it may be the taking up of life. It may be the torture of wounds; it may perhaps be the greater torture of ministering to the wounds of others. It may be action; it may

[10] Rom. 8:38-39.

be its opposite, inaction and endurance. "Those also serve who only stand and wait."[11] But undoubtedly it will be something, and you will not be consulted as to what it shall be.

Does the prospect appall you? If it does, very well. But be assured there is no other road to the real understanding of love. If it does not; if, in spite of the dread, there is still hope and courage; if you can still say that love can find strength to do whatever love may demand; if you wish to know by experience the meaning of love, then make your preparations. Put a check upon self-seeking, on self-gratification, on looking for reward, and you will have cleared the ground. Be led by something more than mere argument, mere reasoning of your own, that dead and fallacious thing that is the offspring of man's short sight. See without turning aside the compelling force of truth in itself, of nobility in itself, of beauty in itself, of goodness in itself, wherever these may be found. Submit to them without drawing back; be guided by them without flinching.

And lastly, when the spirit is moved to act, to give itself for something noble, to follow the light, to do that

[11] John Milton.

which is in itself worth doing, then let it go. Do not hesitate; do not keep it in fetters; do not too much count the cost. Do not tremble at the danger; or if you do, for you cannot always help it, set your teeth and step forward. "He that putteth his hand to the plough and looketh back is not worthy of me."[12]

These are the exercises by which the power to love may be developed. On such ground, under such training, love will grow; of that you need not doubt. For the germ of love is in every human heart. The pity of it is that, in some, it is nipped and frostbitten before it has had time to come to maturity.

But foster the spark, and it will enkindle. At first, it will thrill you with its glow. You will know it by its heat, by the ease with which it aids you to face a trouble, by the joy you find in doing. But later, be prepared for sacrifice. When the flower has bloomed and the fruit is setting, then, gardeners tell us, is the time of trial. When you have made a certain way, and you have laughed and sung along the road, then will love begin to lead through darker ways, and whither you do not wish to go. It will ask of you surrenders for which you had not bargained.

[12] Cf. Luke 9:62.

Determine whether your love is true

It will disappoint you. It will fail to recognize you when you come face-to-face. It will leave your noblest actions unrequited, the noblest powers of your soul undeveloped. It will misinterpret your best motives, will envy your worthiest deeds, will crush you with sarcasm, and will embitter you with mistrust and suspicion and dislike and an assumption of contempt. At critical moments, it will turn its back upon you and will ignore you when you are down. If you appeal for help, it will cry out against you. It will see you wounded on the road and pass you by; crucified, and say it was only your desert; dripping your life's blood out, and coldly wait the end.

And then, when it has killed you, you will come to know. "He that loses his life for my sake shall find it."[13] When it has purified you, when there is left not a spark of that mean thing self, when you no longer look for relief, for consolation, for comfort, but only for strength to go on, then will come the revelation. Then you will know that which, by any other training, eye can never see, nor ear hear, nor can it enter into the heart of man to conceive.[14]

[13] Matt. 16:25.
[14] 1 Cor. 2:9.

Chapter Two

❧

Find God
in your loneliness

Every profession requires special training. Besides special powers and talents, besides special instruction, we may almost say it requires special virtues. The virtues most needful for a successful physician are not precisely those required for a successful lawyer. One will have patience with the body of a man; the other will have patience with his ways. From both of these, a soldier differs in almost every particular; perhaps he most of all needs patience with himself.

The same is true of an apostle, of whatever kind he may be; he, too, must have his special qualifications. Priest or layman, religious or secular, man or woman, old or young, if God would make apostles of them, there is one school through which one and all must pass, one certificate they must all acquire. And when He is determined that they shall be apostles, He puts them through this school, whether they choose it or not.

Spiritual Excellence

It is a school very different from that in which the world develops its ideal. When it has the making of a man in hand, above all when it would make him one who is to understand and have influence over others, its first and foremost object is to give him what it calls experience of men. He is sent out to see the world, to mix with his fellowmen, to learn the art of dealing with them, of enjoying their company, and of bending their lives; and it almost foretells the extent of his future plane of action by the measure of the knowledge he has gained.

Not so are the ways of God. He has other means of giving an apostle power over other men; indeed, it is the very opposite. "The weak things of this world God hath chosen to confound the strong,"[15] said the greatest of apostles; and by "the weak things" he meant not only the weakest instruments, but the methods that men most ignore. And of all methods, perhaps none is more ignored by man as a race, and by man as an individual, than the method of loneliness.

To most men, loneliness is a doom. It is imposed upon a criminal as the heaviest of punishments. Carried

[15] 1 Cor. 1:27.

to extremes, we know, it will drive him mad. Nothing seems so to unman a man as the loneliness of a prison cell.

Even for those who are not criminals, nothing so wrings pity from a human heart as the sight of another who is utterly alone. Loneliness to many is the very ghost of life, dogging their steps, haunting them at every turn, from which they are always trying to escape. It cannot be fought, it cannot be avoided, yet there is nothing many more dread for themselves or see with more concern in others.

Yet it is this very thing that God has chosen to be the school of training for His own. He has shown it without possibility of mistake. Look down the line of the Old Testament, and you will find it written everywhere. At this distance of time and space, it is not easy for us to distinguish the details. We see in history the broad effects of lives; we do not always read between the lines and detect the causes that those effects imply. But we have only to hold our gaze steady, to wait for the haze to lift, and this detail at least will grow upon us.

Abraham: what was he but a model of loneliness? "In those days, God said to Abraham: Leave thy country and thy father's house, and come into a land which I shall show thee."[16] Moses, the savior of his people, must first be brought up in an alien's house and must then be made perfect in a wilderness. David was a lonely man. Not otherwise could he have known the depth of soul that cried out in his lament for the loss of Saul and Jonathan; not otherwise could he have learned to endure and love on when friend and foe alike turned against him. And the prophets, the giants of the latter age, Amos and Osee, Isaias and Jeremias, Ezechiel and Daniel: what are they but gaunt, lonely figures, standing out upon the distant skyline, with the red light of a setting sun behind them? Last of all comes the Baptist, the man of all men lonely, bestriding the gulf that separates two worlds, who, because of his momentous mission, must be alone from his childhood.

If, in the days of God's manifest guidance, this was true, no less is it true in the days of hidden grace. Our Lord Himself was alone; in the wilderness of humanity He lived so long a time, and men did not know Him. "He was in the world, and the world knew Him not; He came unto His own, and His own received Him not."[17]

[16] Cf. Gen. 12:1.
[17] John 1:10-11.

His fellow Nazarenes claimed to know Him, and did not. His enemies knew Him and refused to own it. His friends — at one point in His life, "many went back and walked no more with Him";[18] at another, "all fled away";[19] at the very end, He had to say, "How long a time have I been with you, and have you not known me?"[20] He was born deserted; He lived alone; He died a lonely criminal's death. And if we want proof that He felt it, we have it, first, in His frequent cries of pain, and second, in the eager way He grasped at and rewarded every mark of companionship offered Him.

As with the Master, so it was with the disciple. St. Paul's aloneness begins with his conversion. When he rose from his bed and his blindness, God took him "into a silent place apart," to the desert of Arabia, and there He "spoke to his soul." And since his time, what has been the tale of every saint's life but one of a lonely heart, separated and hedged around, "a garden enclosed, a fountain sealed up"[21] — above all, of such saints as were

[18] John 6:67 (RSV = John 6:66).
[19] Mark 14:50.
[20] John 14:9.
[21] Cant. 4:12 (RSV = Song of Sol. 4:12).

called to do a great life's work in the midst of men? We think of Cistercians and Carthusians, of Carmelites and Poor Clares, and fancy that their lives are buried all alone in their cloisters; those who know have not very far to seek to find lonelier lives than theirs. Francis Xavier,[22] to take but a single instance — how far more alone he stands, in the welter of human life in the midst of which he lived, than does St. Bruno[23] himself on his lonely mountainside!

So does God deal with His own — above all, with those of His own whom He has chosen to use for others. And the reason is not hard to discover. There are three schools of suffering, each with its own special blessing to bestow: physical, mental, and the inner school that lies behind them both: loneliness of soul. Physical suffering makes for tenderness of heart and a patient judgment. Mental suffering gives a deepened sympathy, an active influence that, when "lifted up, draws all things to itself."[24]

[22] St. Francis Xavier (1506-1552), Jesuit missionary to the East Indies.

[23] St. Bruno (1030-1101), founder of the Carthusian Order.

[24] Cf. John 12:32.

Find God in your loneliness

But loneliness of soul does more than this; it gives independence and strength. Even in the natural plane, it secures liberty of spirit, it develops clearness of judgment, and it enforces power of will. But this is by no means all. In the Old Testament, Wisdom is heard to say, "Come with me into a silent place apart, and I will speak to thy soul"; and no one who has heard the calling of the Holy Spirit can misunderstand what this means: the deafness to His voice that may be caused by the din of men, and the clear ring that is given to His words when they come to us across the desert through the night. Loneliness of soul gives wisdom — that breadth of vision that belongs to him who sees the entire valley from the hilltop. Loneliness of soul gives understanding — that further power of seeing beneath the surfaces of life. Loneliness of soul gives counsel to sustain another, and fortitude to endure its own burden. All the seven gifts of the Holy Spirit[25] come through and are fostered by loneliness of soul.

These are some of the fruits of this special school of suffering. Nonetheless, let it not be forgotten that a

[25] Wisdom, understanding, knowledge, counsel, fortitude, piety, and fear of the Lord.

school of suffering it is. We are not speaking here of the loneliness that is a joy and a comfort, in which, as the popular phrase goes, we are "never less alone than when alone." We are speaking of that sense of desertion, of alienation from our kindred, of being somehow out of joint with all the world, of separation from God Himself, which human nature can scarcely endure, which even our Lord Himself considered to justify a cry for relief.[26] Physical suffering He foresaw for His disciples, but He merely bade them rejoice at the prospect. Mental suffering He also promised them; this, again, they were to take as a sign that His blessing was upon them. But loneliness of soul He treats quite differently. Its agony He fully recognizes; He is not afraid to let them see its effect upon Him. In the garden, on the Cross, His cries had almost scandalized posterity. And as for His whole life: an angel lost and broken-winged in this poor world would be a pitiable, lonely thing; what then must have been the loneliness of the exiled Son of God?

Then, having "given us an example," having justified, as it were, our complaining by His own, He proceeds to soothe the bitterness for those who must undergo it.

[26] Matt. 27:46.

"My little children," He calls them, on the eve of the great Day of Loneliness. "Let not your heart be troubled," He says, "nor let it be afraid. . . . It is expedient for you that I go, for if I go not, the Spirit will not come to you."[27] And He bribes them to go through with it because of all that is to follow. Last of all, He assures them that it will not be all desertion: "I will not leave you orphans; I will come to you. Now indeed you have sorrow, but I will see you again, and your heart shall rejoice; and your joy no man shall take from you."[28] Then, as if to support Himself by the same argument by which He supports them, He concludes, "Behold the hour cometh, and it is now come, that you shall be scattered every man to his own, and shall leave me alone: and yet I am not alone, because the Father is with me."[29]

Nowhere has Christ our Lord come nearer to us than in His loneliness and ours. Nowhere has He shown Himself more human. Nowhere has He more condoned the cry of pain, the appeal for some relief. Nowhere has He done more, by example and by promise, to nerve us

[27] Cf. John 14:27; 16:7.
[28] John 14:18; 16:22.
[29] John 16:32.

to endurance. And who that has tried does not know the truth of His promise? St. Paul speaks for such as these, and they echo his words, which have for them a meaning all their own: "I am sure that neither death, nor life, nor angels, nor principalities, nor powers, nor things present, nor things to come, nor might, nor height, nor depth, nor any other creature shall be able to separate me from the love of God, which is in Christ Jesus our Lord."

Chapter Three

~

Hunger for the things of Heaven

There is one characteristic common to all great souls, whether they are good or evil, in whatever sphere they may be found. It is seen in a Byron, or a Shelley, or a Goethe, in an Alexander, a Caesar, a Napoleon, in a Luther, a Calvin, a Wesley, in a Paul, a Xavier, a Teresa. In some, it attains to some issue, although never to a complete satisfaction; in others, it seems only to add to the tragedy of life, rendering it broken-winged and desperate. This common characteristic is a certain craving to be something more than merely ordinary, to do something more than it is given to everyone to do, to attain to some end above the common. This alone seems to them to justify life. As Robert Browning has put it, "A man's reach should be beyond his grasp / Or what's a Heaven for?"

One man will endeavor to satisfy this craving in words. He will dive through life itself and fathom its depths; he will disclose its pearls or its weeds as the case may be. Such a man we call either a poet or a philosopher, or both.

Another will express it in action. He will set out to conquer nations or to govern them. He will make himself a leader of men for good or for evil. Such we call a general or a statesman.

A third is roused to remedy the evils of his time, whether they are real or imagined, religious, political, or social. He forms his theory; he has his own end in view; he multiplies his following. For good or for evil, his mark on the world is permanent. Such a man we call a reformer, or a revolutionist, as the case may be.

Yet a fourth is filled with a craving for that which no deed, or triumph, or reform in the world can give him. He hungers for that which is beyond the world's edge. He must leap out to it, grasp it, and live the life of man toward it. For this end, every sacrifice in this world is a negligible quantity. Such a man we call a saint, at least such are the foundations of a saint, and it is on this account that the saints are the greatest among mankind.

They are, we assert, the greatest men among mankind, even judged by man's own standards. For if greatness consists in the violence of one's craving, the object toward which it tends, and the force with which it is followed, then the saints compare with and surpass all the greatest heroes in the world. In other men, the range is avowedly confined to this life and all that it contains. For them, the horizon loses itself in the mist of the infinite; their aspirations are infinite in range, infinite in possibilities, and therefore beyond the power of eye to see, or ear to hear, or the heart of man to conceive. Others have human ends; they make use of human means. These make light of what is human. They take its effects as but the byproduct of their labor, and for the means, they "have nothing and possess all things,"[30] "glory in their infirmities, that the power of God may be manifested in them,"[31] take it as their principle that "the weak things of this world hath God chosen to confound the strong."[32]

Thus is this almost infinite craving an essential characteristic of sanctity. Without it, a man would not rise above this world; with it, he becomes the greatest among men. It has two necessary consequences; it explains that

[30] Cf. 2 Cor. 6:10.
[31] Cf. 2 Cor. 12:9.
[32] Cf. 1 Cor. 1:27.

paradox, that consciousness at once of success and failure, which seems to run through the lives of all the saints, and indeed of all who, although not saints, nevertheless aspire after sanctity. Their cravings make them do greater things than it is given to less hungry hearts to do; these same cravings make them dissatisfied with all that they have done, so that in the end they can only cry out, "I am a useless servant!"[33] The humility of the saint, such a contradiction to those who look on from the outside, is no contradiction in itself; it is only a recognition of the vast difference between all that he accomplishes and the glorious ideal that he has before him.

Let us look at this a little more closely, for it touches perhaps the darkest spot in the lives of many.

It is of the essence of growth of any kind to become disillusioned. A child is delighted with his toys; he grows and immediately discards them. He has been disillusioned. A boy revels in a certain kind of story; he grows and tends to pity those who understand no more. A youth is keen to excel in sports or games; he grows, and only the battlefield or the government of men will satisfy him. And with the spiritual-minded man it is the

[33] Cf. Luke 17:10.

same. He may have reveled in the enjoyment of this life, and even for a time have found it sufficient. But one day he begins to grow. He discovers there are more things in Heaven and earth than are dreamed of in this world's philosophy. His knowledge of the more and greater things creates some disgust for the little things around him, with which, nevertheless, so long as he lives, his life must be filled up. He is a little disillusioned, exactly as the child, the boy, and the youth. And the consequent sense of disappointment, or failure, he may easily take for more than he should.

Again, the spiritual-minded man cannot but be of an ardent nature. Keen to appreciate, he is also keen to love. And, while he grows, until his love has found its final goal, he will more than once experience the disillusion of love that has been ill-bestowed. He will bestow it where it is not deserved, deceived by some little outward show. He will give it, and it will not be returned. He will pour it out and will find that the cup that should have received it could hold so much and no more.

And meanwhile his own heart will be growing. It will yearn for something more worthy, for the best thing that may be loved. It will reach out into the infinite, both of giving and of receiving. When it has gone thus far, when it has drunk of the best and worthiest that this life has to give, and has found it wanting, when more is not received, when the little that it had is taken away, by death, by separation, by faithlessness, by misunder-standing, or by whatever cause, when the ordinary in-terests of flattened-out life absorb its time and powers, but have no place for the affections, there grows a sense of loss, of disappointment, which the hungry victim may too often mistake for failure.

Or third, there is the result of that reaction which comes from experience, and this is of two kinds. There is the bitter discovery that men and things are not al-ways the ideals that he had pictured in his mind. This world, and every man in this world, is capable of so much, might be so much, if only . . . And the "if only" is frustrated by so many trifles, or else, apparently, by so much that God, if He would, could arrange! Sometimes individuals will not see what is good; sometimes, seeing, they will not follow. Sometimes a good thing, to us so clear, is contested, opposed, or thwarted by others, ap-parently no less eager than we in the service of God. Sometimes it is circumstances that hinder any possibil-ity of action. Sometimes it is those in authority who seem to hinder. Sometimes there is actual scandal and corruption where nothing but zeal and sacrifice should reign. In a thousand ways, we "live and learn"; and it needs a patient and a persevering heart to remain loyal under the process. It begins to suspect its own cravings; perhaps it begins to resign itself to a lower satisfaction.

The second kind is the experience of ourselves. From time to time in our lives, the supernatural gains a strong hold upon us. There are periods, longer or shorter, for which we can account or cannot, when we seem to awaken to a new revelation; when we see things we never saw before, when prayer suddenly becomes a new light, at once satisfying and easy, when efforts to live a nobler life are full of inspiration, when we scarcely touch the ground beneath us on our way to God, when we tell ourselves, with some enthusiasm, that now "we have found Him whom our soul loveth; we have held Him and will not let Him go";[34] that henceforth "nothing shall separate us from the love which we have in Christ Jesus, our Lord."

Then suddenly, or perhaps it may be gradually, all this passes away. The revelation grows dim in the distance, remaining as a recollection and no more. Prayer

[34] Cf. Cant. 3:4 (RSV = Song of Sol. 3:4).

becomes again the humdrum affair it was of old, if it does not sink even lower. Effort becomes impossible, progress is none, the burden of this life and its myriad temptations press on us, and we walk with leaden shackles on our feet.

At once we are troubled and distressed. We compare our present state with our last and discover what we call a falling off. We cannot help making the contrast, and it needs both effort and understanding not to draw a seemingly obvious conclusion. If once we prayed well, and now the least prayer is a weary labor, we presume that this proves our own shortcomings. If we could record daily victories before, and now we have nothing but defeats, this we take as clear evidence that we are wholly wanting. If now we are obsessed on every side with temptations of every nature, and once we had sailed into the open sea with nothing but a straight course before us, we tell ourselves that we have gone back. Our heart becomes hungrier than ever. Having once tasted "how sweet is the Lord,"[35] it can never be satisfied with anything less; and it takes its dissatisfaction for an evil sign.

[35] Cf. Ps. 33:9 (RSV = Ps. 34:8).

In reality, it is the opposite. A hungry heart is, as we have said, the foundation of a saintly heart. It is the heart that is settled and contented that kills its cravings and satisfies its hunger with the husks that lie about. It is such a heart that should make us uneasy. And God so loves a hungry heart that He will stir the hunger in a hundred ways. One of these is to give it just a taste of "the things that are more excellent,"[36] and then to take them away.

Let us not be mistaken. Let us not misinterpret ourselves. Let us rejoice that we are made so to hunger and thirst for justice, for we shall have our fill.[37]

Chapter Four

❧

*Learn to overcome
common hindrances
to prayer*

A child never complains of being unable to pray. Complaints are seldom made by older people to whom prayer is not an ordinary thing or a well-known experience. It is only those who have learned something of the meaning and life of prayer that complain of the difficulty they find in it. One might almost go further and assert the seeming paradox that the more we know about prayer, the more difficult it tends to become.

Of course, prayer is a gift of God, and His gifts are free and may not be purchased. Nonetheless, of all His gifts, perhaps none is more nearly purchasable than prayer — none that He more willingly gives in return for what we offer Him. More than any other of His gifts, the gift of prayer depends on our desire for it, our efforts to attain it, and the dispositions we prepare for its reception.

Hence, while we must allow that God can and often does bestow the gift of prayer, and consolation in prayer, and life in prayer, of His own overflowing bounty and without consideration of previous dispositions, still it is also true that ordinarily, and ultimately for all, certain dispositions must always be preserved if the habit of, and interest in, and relish for prayer are to be maintained. Prayer is a delicate flower that needs to be guarded and tended. If we wish to have it in full bloom, we must look well to it, both in its growth and in its heyday, and in all its surroundings.

What, then, are some of the precautions we should take? They are best learned by each one from his own experience. There is no other road to prayer — not what we have read in books or what we have heard from others, but exactly as much as we have learned from ourselves, and no more.

Here at least may be suggested a few preliminary warnings. When we examine our prayer or our failure in it, the first thing we usually have to say is that our minds have been far afield. We began well enough — or we did not, which is much more common than we are always willing to allow — but almost immediately we were lost. People we know wandered through our brain — above all, two classes: those we like best and those we like least. With the former, we built our castles in the clouds; the latter we pelted with torrents of abuse and saw ourselves in imagination triumphantly stamping on their prostrate forms. Or events of the past, or imaginary events of the future, turned themselves over and over, distorted themselves, mixed themselves up, and usually left us either humbled at our proneness to evil, or grumbling at somebody's imagined injustice toward us. Let us humbly confess it: this or such as this is often the total of our morning meditation.

Or we find we have taken up a restful position of body. We are rather more than usually tired — how many mornings are we not able to say this? We are afraid of straining ourselves by a long vigil; we recall the warning of St. Teresa that no one can pray whose body is in torture. Besides, we have so often found, or at least we tell ourselves that we have often found, that a restful attitude conduces to prayer. But, as a matter of fact, whatever may be the prayer of the first half-minute, the restful attitude has led to an absolute blank. It has either soothed us into slumber or else has let our minds go wandering away to the moon. The end comes, and we find ourselves, in body, mind, and soul, exactly where we were when we sat down or reclined. Of how many morning meditations is this the history?

Spiritual Excellence

There is yet a third experience. It often happens that, much as we desire and relish the thought of spiritual things at other times, in time of prayer this desire and this relish seem utterly to vanish. There succeeds nothing but weariness and languor. Mean and shameful thoughts come careening through our brain that at other times are wholly absent. And we have scarcely begun our prayer when we long with an almost irresistible longing for the end. Any distraction becomes welcome; any excuse for limiting the time allotted is acceptable. Instead of being the desire of our hearts, the time of prayer becomes the time of almost intolerable torture.

These are three common experiences, which are perhaps the tale of the prayer of many, and from which very few indeed escape. But fortunately they have their remedy written right across them. We have but to acknowledge them. We have to discover the right relation that exists between prayer and mortification; we have to see that, to some extent at least, one is the price of the other and to see how far and in what coin that price must be paid.

For, in the first place, if excessive preoccupation is a hindrance to prayer, we must train ourselves, especially before the time of prayer, to resist this preoccupation.

Overcome common hindrances to prayer

This does not, or at least need not, mean that we must do less work than before, or that we must be less interested in it, or that we must pay less attention to it than to ourselves. The example of all the saints of prayer — witness St. Francis Xavier, St. Teresa, St. Vincent de Paul[38] — is evidence in abundance that prayer never hinders work. But it does mean that no matter how much, or how engrossing, or how urgent the work may be, it must never be allowed to master us. We must never let ourselves become the slaves of our surroundings or our circumstances. We must educate the mind by severe discipline. If necessary, we must say to everything that threatens to engross and overwhelm us, "Thus far and no further." The mind must learn to shut the door to interference, to preserve its command of its own castle. This is the active side of the virtue known as peace of mind, and such discipline, such mortification, will teach us to command our thoughts and affections in time of prayer.

Second, if, after an honest self-examination, bodily ease is found to be a hindrance to prayer, then not in

[38] St. Vincent de Paul (1580-1660), founder of the Lazarist Fathers and the Sisters of Charity.

time of prayer only, but at other times also, we must train the body to give up its comfort for the sake of energy of mind and heart. It is not enough to wait until the time of prayer comes to begin our educating of the body; then, not only are the reasons for relaxation more urgent and apparent, but the habit of always yielding tells heavily against us. Lazy-bodied people at ordinary times have no sufficient vigor with which to resist laziness of body in time of prayer. On the other hand, a little sacrifice at other times, gradual inuring of ourselves not to have absolutely all the comfort that our bodies seek, reacts in prayer and gives us the physical strength to resist this second hindrance.

Third, if, as we have said, nature resists the supernatural effort to be made in prayer, if prayer time is a time of weariness and agony, then there are three things to be done; for, let it be noticed, this is a hindrance to prayer much more likely to come from without than from within, much more likely to be a real trial than merely a consequence of our own unfaithfulness and self-indulgence.

First, at other times that are not strictly times of prayer, when your spirit is moved to pray — to utter a brief, spontaneous prayer, to answer the ringing of the

Angelus,[39] or to pay a visit to the Blessed Sacrament — let it not be too easily thwarted. Let it be allowed to pray when nature does not seem to be in conflict; gradually nature itself will learn to "taste and see how sweet is the Lord."

Again, when prayer is irksome, when body and soul are weary, if prayer is not a matter of duty, it is of little use driving the soul against its own inclination. To pray long at such times, simply because we have made up our mind to do so, only makes prayer a matter of greater horror; and this warning we have from perhaps the greatest student of the human soul, St. Ignatius of Loyola. Long devotions at such times, carried out because they are long, may easily break the spirit and turn it away from prayer altogether.

On the other hand, when prayer is a duty, when the prayers we say are those which belong to our state of life or are appointed by our rule, our practice must be the exact opposite. We must then not clip the time, but we must train ourselves to prolong it. And the reason is

---

[39] At six o'clock a.m., noon, and six o'clock p.m., some churches ring a bell to call the faithful to pray the *Angelus*, a prayer that recalls the Incarnation.

that prayer is then something more than a matter of inclination. It is the fulfillment of a duty; and no yielding in duty can possibly make for growth in prayer.

These, then, are three common hindrances to prayer, very often overlooked, and yet stunting prayer at its outset, and three remedies by which they may be met. Of course, it may be, and for the fervent it often is, that apparent failure in prayer is due to other causes. With all the best will and effort and preparation in the world, we may still seem to make little progress; the trial may come entirely from the hand of God. Nevertheless, it is possible that even this may depend upon the shortcomings of which we have spoken far more than we at first suspect. We may be making many efforts in many ways, and yet in some conscious particular we may know that we are wholly yielding to ourselves. In any case, we can go no further until the first evils have been cured; and in matter of fact, God always in the end, or from time to time, rewards and encourages consistent effort enough and more than enough to make us feel that it has been worthwhile.

Hence, to sum up the duty of the man of prayer: discipline or control of thought, discipline or control of body, discipline or control of nature. We might well add a fourth, which might be called discipline of heart, for here, too, is a serious, even a fatal, hindrance to prayer. We do not like to own it; we scarcely have the courage to face the consequence. Still, disordered affection, giving too much of ourselves to any creature whatsoever, caring too much for anyone or anything, is often a cause of failure in prayer that would otherwise be good. Human nature refuses to acknowledge it; it looks for any other cause; it will even ascribe it to its own wickedness. But if we wish to learn to pray, we must be quite true to ourselves and in this matter most of all.

Chapter Five

❧

Do not limit yourself
to certain forms
of prayer

~

Both St. Teresa and St. John of the Cross,[40] the great teachers of prayer, lament, not so much that people do not pray more, but that they do not make more advancement in prayer. They tell us very plainly that prayer is a science as well as a practice; that if we will only go the right way about it, we shall learn astonishingly both what prayer itself is and what wonderful things it has to reveal; and that there is no one, man or woman, educated or uneducated, religious or secular, who cannot come to at least some knowledge, much more than most of us usually achieve.

But, alas, they add, there are few who make much advancement; few get beyond the most elementary principles. And the chief reasons are either that they will

[40] St. John of the Cross (1542-1591), Carmelite mystic and reformer of the Carmelite Order.

not persevere, or that they fear to let themselves go forward, or that they have no one to show them the way to proceed.

Now, it is not for anyone to presume to set himself up as a guide in prayer, much less as a universal guide, for prayer is an individual thing. It is the individual's relationship with God, and God has His own way of dealing with individuals. Nevertheless, there are certain elementary truths, not realized by all, yet easily discovered by one who has had much to do with prayer, whether in his own soul or in others. Once accepted, these truths will at once clear away many obstacles for any soul that wishes to progress in prayer. To mention a few of these may be useful; it may give a little light to some who walk in darkness and who may already have become despondent about their prayer, finding, as no doubt they do, that it falls so short of their desires and ambitions, finding it so disappointing.

In the first place, then, let it be remembered that prayer does not consist in merely saying prayers. Prayer, from its definition, is "the raising of the mind and heart to God," and there are many more ways, sometimes better ways, of doing this than by repeating forms of prayer, however good. Forms of prayer are good insofar as they do this for us and no further: they help us to put into words the thoughts of our mind and the feelings of our heart. But if those thoughts and feelings can be taught to express themselves spontaneously, even without any words at all, or at least with very few, our prayer is better than that which depends upon a form.

"But I am afraid to give up the form. That at least ties me down to something clear and definite. If I gave up the form, and relied on my own thoughts and feelings and expression, these may someday fail me, and then I would be without any prayer at all." This objection is a good one; a proof that it is a good one is that it is very common, very real, and obviously comes from those who wish to do their best. Still, it is an objection and no more, and is one of the chief hindrances to progress in prayer.

For clearly what is our own is better than what we substitute in its place. Even if our words are more faulty, or our expression more vague, what comes straight from the heart is better than all else. When we read the New Testament and hear the poor man on the roadside merely crying, "Lord, help me!";[41] or St. Peter breaking down

---

[41] Cf. Luke 18:38.

with "Lord, thou knowest that I love Thee";[42] or St. Thomas paralyzed into his "My Lord, and my God!";[43] or our Lord Jesus Himself unable to do more than repeat the self-same words "Father, if it be possible, let this chalice pass from me,"[44] then we know that we are listening to the truest prayer. And when, in like manner, in our own turn we find our own hearts crying out to God, whether in faith, or love, or hope, or contrition, or oblation, or anything else, we should know that our prayer is of our best, even a minute of which crying is more precious than another prayer of many words.

The first hint, then, to be given to one who wishes to make progress in prayer is that the soul should not confine itself so as to be tied down to a formula, however good. Suppose, for example, that I am accustomed to take a quarter of an hour, in preparation for or thanksgiving after Communion. And suppose that to fill up this time I have a fixed set of prayers that I repeat. I may someday find — and, if I try, I most certainly shall find — that while repeating the prayers, or even before,

[42] John 21:17.
[43] John 20:28.
[44] Matt. 26:39.

Do not limit yourself to forms of prayer

I am impelled to dwell on one word, or one idea, or one strong feeling of the heart. I am drawn to say, "Jesus!" in welcome and to dwell upon the name, or to be sorry that I receive Him so poorly, or whatever else. Shall I entertain this feeling at the expense of my set of prayers, or must I keep my rule and say them?

The answer should be clear: keep the time, not the form of words. If I speak heart-to-heart with God even for two minutes, my prayer is deeper, and will tell more deeply on me, than the words of another; and I shall learn soon how from that small beginning God will draw me forward and teach me more. If I am true to the appointed time, I need not fear the danger that the objection suggests. And when I find that my mind wanders, or my heart is cold and unmoved, I can always fall back on my set prayers to fill up the time that remains.

Only let us be simple and genuine in our prayer, and we shall soon discover the value of this "liberty of the children of God";[45] for forms of prayer, excellent and constantly useful as they are, are best when they suggest this deeper praying of our own, not when they chain us down to their repetition. Even the best prayers, if merely

[45] Cf. Rom. 8:21.

repeated and not lingered over, will in time become a weary formula. And which of us has not gone through the experience of outgrowing some form of prayer, and yet sometimes we are afraid to set it aside?

But such prayerfulness as is here suggested is always alive, and if the form is in consequence less often said, it has given way to something far more fruitful. I would rather say, "Jesus, I love You," for an hour, if I could mean it all the time, than repeat or read the most perfect act of love composed by the greatest saint or the most consummate poet. My words would be fewer, and weaker, and more stammering; but Jesus would know that at least they are mine and no other's — the words of "an infant crying in the night. / An infant crying for the light. / And with no language but a cry"[46] — and I think He would hear them more tenderly.

Hence, the first practical hint to be given to one who sincerely wishes to learn how to pray is that we should be faithful to our time of prayer rather than to our words. Prayer cannot easily be measured by words; it is measured best by earnestness of purpose, depth of meaning, and intensity of feeling. And by feeling is not

[46] Alfred Tennyson, *In Memoriam*.

meant our sentiment, but the reality behind it that abides in our heart.

This is the method by which, on his own confession, St. Aloysius Gonzaga[47] grew to be so great a man of prayer. He began with the form, like the rest of us; gradually the form was made to yield to the feelings of his heart that it evoked; in the end we find him writing and developing forms of his own. And the same may be said of many others, conspicuous saints of prayer on the one hand, and, on the other, hidden souls of prayer who know God and His Christ by an intimate experience all their own.

Let us take an example. A certain lady, who gave much of her time and her wealth to the poor, chanced in her rounds to come across an old woman in a humble cottage who had been bedridden for years. She sat by the sufferer's side, gave her what comfort she could, and then asked her about her prayers.

"Do you say your Rosary every day?" she asked.

"Every day? Bless you no, not every day, Madame. I haven't always time" was the answer.

---

[47] St. Aloysius Gonzaga (1568-1591), Jesuit who ministered to plague victims.

Not always time! Yet the old woman was lying there all day long and every day, often with no one to visit her for hours together!

"Why, what do you do with your time?" the lady naturally asked.

"Well, Madame," said the poor victim, "when I first broke my thigh and was told I would never rise from my bed again, I just thought I would give myself to my prayers. So I arranged some prayers that I would say every day, and some I would say at intervals. And to make them go better, I would say them very slowly. But soon the Our Father began to grow and grow, until now it sometimes takes me the whole week to get through it. Oh, Madame, if people only knew what was in the Our Father!"

And here the poor, uneducated old woman broke into an exposition of the prayer, the nature of the Fatherhood of God, and His attitude toward us, His children, such, as the lady herself told me, as might have come from the lips of the most highly trained saint and theologian.

And perhaps they did — but from a saint and theologian trained in God's own school, the school of prayer combined with welcome suffering.

Do not limit yourself to forms of prayer

This, incidentally, reminds us of two other truths: first, that suffering is not wholly evil, however much we may fear it; and second, that prayer and suffering are seldom far removed, but that both give strength, depth, and fruitfulness to one another.

Chapter Six

∽

Speak to God
from your heart

We have made an attempt to let souls understand that often enough the chief hindrance to progress in prayer is just our own way of praying. We cling sometimes too much to our adopted forms of prayer, good as they are in themselves, and so chain down our mind and heart, preventing them from raising themselves spontaneously to God.

Let it never be forgotten that spontaneous prayer, straight from the heart, however feebly it is worded, is always better than prayer of form and is always likely to lead to higher things. Fixed forms are good, and are even necessary, because often enough the soul is unable to express itself. But when the soul can express itself, let it do so, speaking to God face-to-face so far as it is permitted.

We come now to a second consideration that naturally follows from the first, and it is this: If our own expression of our hearts in prayer is better than any other, and if our own expression of ourselves never wears out or becomes a mere form, whereas other kinds, however good, are liable to be outgrown, it is important that the soul should train itself in self-expression in prayer, so that sufficient words may come spontaneously to it. This is one of the great values of brief, spontaneous prayers, and of short phrases from the Scripture, such as "My Lord and my God,"[48] "Jesus, Son of David, have mercy on me,"[49] "For thou, O Lord, art sweet and gentle, and of much mercy to all who hope in Thee," "Lord, Thou knowest all things; Thou knowest that I love Thee."[50] Phrases such as these crystallize our thoughts, and our heart, when it endeavors to leap up to God, finds in them an easy and spontaneous form of speech. These, then, should be collected and often used. And there is no man or woman in the world, however "unspiritual," however preoccupied with business, who cannot practice this method, anywhere, everywhere, and realize its benefit.

[48] John 20:28.
[49] Luke 18:38.
[50] John 21:17.

For some, indeed, this form of prayer, once adopted, abundantly suffices. It leads of itself to almost everything else. For others, it is easier to train the soul in self-expression by means of definite acts:

- *Of faith:* "Lord, I believe; help my unbelief."[51]

- *Of hope:* "In Thee, O Lord, I have hoped, let me not be confounded forever."[52]

- *Of humility:* "Lord, I am not worthy that Thou shouldst enter under my roof."[53]

- *Of contrition:* "Father, I have sinned against Heaven and before Thee."[54]

And so on. This method is usually better than the last, chiefly because there is less danger of wandering, one act naturally leading to another.

But in order that this form of prayer may be made most fruitfully, it is always good to make some plan beforehand of the road we propose to follow. Thus, before

[51] Mark 9:23 (RSV = Mark 9:24).
[52] Cf. Ps. 30:2 (RSV = Ps. 31:1).
[53] Luke 7:6.
[54] Luke 15:18.

Spiritual Excellence

Communion, we may say to ourselves, "Today I will exercise myself in faith, hope, and charity." In a visit to the Blessed Sacrament, we may propose, "I will make acts of humility, contrition, and love in His presence." On a journey, in a car, during a spare ten minutes, we may begin, "I will make an act of the presence of God to me, and of my presence to Him, and let my heart speak to Him as my companion." We need not always keep to the arrangement, but such preparation as this is splendid training, not only for prayer, but also in the very important matter of self-control in all things.

Still, there are some with whom even this form of prayer will not always be satisfying. There come times when no outward words will sufficiently express the depth of feeling in the soul; it must speak for itself or not at all. Especially is this the case when we are impressed with the sense of our own nothingness, or when the misery of sin, especially of our own sins, is deeply realized, or again, as a reaction to, or consequence of this, when we yearn for a better way of living, greater truth, and greater self-surrender.

To such we can only suggest a kind of prayer, a model upon which the soul may work for itself, climbing to God by means of a ladder of its own making. The method is to hold its thoughts steady, taking one at a time without confusion, letting one lead to another naturally, and as slowly as the soul will go, so that it may draw from each step all the fruit that it may be able.

Let us consider some examples, but let it be remembered that these are examples and no more. They are not given merely to be read. They are an effort to show how the soul may guide itself in prayer; how much prayer may be expressed in few words. They are simply a suggestion of the way a soul may, as it were, steady itself in its upward flight.

Let us take a prayer of appeal to our Lady. The soul comes into her presence. It is conscious of her, of itself, and also of the hunger that is gnawing at its heart. Then spontaneously the expressions come, one succeeding the other, slowly, but easily, crystallizing each new feeling as it takes form, and holding it until the soul is satisfied. The prayer may take such shape as the following:

∽

A Visit to Our Lady

Mary, full of grace,
Mary, Mother of God,

Spiritual Excellence

Mary, my Mother,
you are God's perfect creature.
You know me well,
and love me very fondly,
as a mother her most sickly child,
as a mother her most wayward child.
I am weak and sickly.
I am self-willed and wayward.
I want to do better.
I want to be true.
Of myself, I am unable.
My willfulness is too much for me.
My circumstances beat me.
You want to help me, I know,
and you are able.
What, then, prevents you?
Is it anything in myself?
It can be nothing in you.
But what can I do?
I cannot mend myself.
Do it for me.
Take away what hinders you.
I am sincere.
If I am not, I want to be.

Take me at my word.
Be a mother to me.
Firmly but gently,
let me see truly.
Make me be true.
Make me act truly.
Make me worthy of you.

The prayer will then conclude with a Hail Mary, a Hail, Holy Queen,[55] or any other form of prayer according to the choice of our soul.

Or we may draw out a visit to the Blessed Sacrament. We come into the presence of our Lord. We realize Him; we realize ourselves. We have in mind what we wish to express, and the prayer may take a form such as this:

∽

A Visit to the Blessed Sacrament

Jesus,
Jesus Christ,
Jesus, Son of God,

---

[55] The prayers suggested in these pages are included in the appendix.

Spiritual Excellence

Jesus, God made man,
Jesus, truly man,
Jesus, with a greatly loving Heart,
Jesus, here present,
You are.
You love me.
You have proved it wonderfully,
in Your own life and in mine,
in ways I know,
in ways I do not know.
I am a poor creature.
I have done endless harm.
I have hurt You.
I am sorry.
I wish to do better,
but I cannot trust myself.
I seem incapable of any good.
And yet You want me to be Yours, to live with You,
to work with You, to die with You.
You know I cannot do this of myself.
I cannot keep from hurting You.
Yet You pity me and love me — even me.
And you have chosen even me.
So I rely on You.

Speak to God from your heart

I have no other help.
Keep me from doing evil.
Keep me from hurting You.
Make me true in myself.
Make me true to You.
You can if You will,
and if I will.
And I do will so far as I am able.
I have no other hope.
I give You myself,
in spite of, against, my own opposition.

The prayer may conclude with the *Anima Christi*, or any other form of prayer that our soul prefers.

We proceed to give another example, addressed to the first Person of the Blessed Trinity, to whom, after some experience, it is always most easy to pray.

∾

A Prayer to God the Father

My Father.
You are so great.
I am so little.
You are the First and the Last,

Spiritual Excellence

the Beginning and the End.
almighty, everlasting,
and yet my Father.
You made me
the creature that I am,
with my powers and my weaknesses,
because You wanted me — even me.
You put me here.
You gave me this state of life.
You want me back.
I want to be Yours.
I want to do Your work.
When the end comes, I want to go to You,
but without You, I cannot.
You will not fail me.
You cannot fail me.
Let me not fail You.
I know my weakness.
I have learned it from my falls,
which You have permitted,
So that I might learn.
Is it necessary to be taught more?
I can do nothing of myself.
I cannot desire to do anything.

Speak to God from your heart

I cannot keep from harm.
I cannot want to keep from harm.
Help me that I may.
Help me that I may desire it.
Give me the desire for sacrifice —
at least the desire for the desire.
I am an infant asking for bread.
Will my Father give me a stone?

The prayer concludes very naturally with the Our Father, which of itself, treated in a manner like the above, may easily "raise the mind and heart to God" for an hour.

The next illustration is a prayer to the Third Person of the Blessed Trinity — again, a very easy prayer for one who has learned devotion to God the Holy Spirit.

∽

A Prayer to God the Holy Spirit

Holy Spirit of God,
Love of God,
silent, secret, all-preserving,
breathing where You will,
expressing our longings,

Spiritual Excellence

You are wisdom.
You are love.
You are strength and fidelity.
I am none of these.
I need them all.
Sincerely I want them.
I do believe sincerely I want them.
You are the Father of the poor.
You do not fail.
Will You fail me?
Grant that I may never fail You.
I cannot trust myself.
Grant that I may never do wrong,
that I may be wise,
according to my place in life;
that I may love — truly, not falsely;
that I may be faithful
to God, to men;
that I may have strength
sufficient for the task You give me
and may use it.

Let the prayer conclude with the *Veni Creator Spiritus*, or even better with the *Veni Sancte Spiritus*, since the latter, line by line, suggests a continuation of the same simple method.

Lastly, as an example of the way the method may be applied to any of the saints, we may take a prayer to St. Joseph.

❧

A Prayer to St. Joseph

St. Joseph,
the "just man,"
the perfect man of Nazareth,
the spouse of Mary,
the foster-father of Jesus,
the patron of labor,
the patron of a happy death,
the patron of the whole Church,
sinless,
selfless,
unflinchingly generous,
I am a poor beggar.
I am in need.
My tale is against me.
I am very disappointing.

Spiritual Excellence

I have no excuse.
I deserve nothing,
even for the future.
How much can I promise?
I cannot be sure of myself.
But I wish it were otherwise.
I wish to become true,
and you can help me,
for Jesus hears you.
Ask Him to forgive.
Ask Him to forget.
Ask Him to make me sinless, like you,
to make me selfless, like you,
to make me generous.
Take me as your companion
and Mary's
and His.

These examples will suffice to show how the mind may be trained to make its own way in prayer. Such prayer is among the most satisfying to the human soul and is far easier than those who have not tried it may think. But who has not tried it, however unconsciously? For who has not striven at some time to utter to God his soul exactly as it is, and what is the prayer here suggested but this? Let us bear in mind these words of a great saint of prayer: "It is not abundance of knowledge that satisfies the soul, but to feel and relish things internally."

The length of time such a prayer will take is quite indefinite. At one time, when the soul is sluggish or distracted, or when the body is weary, it may be short; at another time, it may easily expand into an hour. In either case, the effort should be made to be very real, to mean exactly what we say, to delay until we are sure that we mean it, speaking to our Lady or to our Lord directly, as to a personal friend in whose presence we are. If this is done, it will soon be found that many more steps can be made between those here suggested, each soul having its particular thoughts, reflections, and manners of expressing its love and contrition.

In general, you may notice that the plan is in each case much the same; indeed, this plan lies at the root of all prayer of colloquy. First comes a realization of the person to whom we pray, with whatever expressions of affection it may evoke; then a realization of ourselves in contrast with this person, with the necessary acts of humility and contrition, or of love and hope; finally, and spontaneously, there is that appeal from one in need to one who possesses an abundance, inspired by a mutual affection that knows it can presume to ask.

Let the actual words be of least account. The realization is the all-important matter. When, with a single, selfless, unaffected heart, we forget to watch our thoughts and words, then the thoughts and words will come of themselves, spontaneously and from the heart.

This last remark suggests a word of warning. We are told by saints who knew much about prayer that we should examine our prayer and see, if we can, what makes us fail. This is very sound advice. No matter what hints may be suggested for prayer, the soundest hint is that we should study our own soul, find the way that it finds easiest and best, and cultivate that as well as we are able. St. Teresa encourages this method; so do many modern teachers of prayer.

At the same time, during the time of prayer itself, there is no distraction more fatal than to reflect and ask ourselves whether we are praying well or not. Such a process is often mere vanity, and vanity is the ruin of all prayer. It kills spontaneity; it stifles fervor. It puts a veil between us and God; it may even substitute us and our own image for Him to whom we wish to pray.

Speak to God from your heart

Let our preparation for prayer be as careful as we like. After prayer, let us ask ourselves what has helped us most and what has been a hindrance. But during prayer, let there be nothing between our heart and God. The great effort of our soul should be toward realization of the truth; and this, if gained even for a moment, as St. Teresa very well says, is worth all the pains that may be taken and bears fruit in great peace of mind.

One last remark may be made in regard to the attitude toward prayer. It is said of St. Ignatius of Loyola that during his busy day, he had little time for long prayer, but that he would find satisfaction in a few moments here and there, whether in his room or before the Blessed Sacrament. But even for these few moments, he would pause before he began. He would not plunge into even so short a prayer without some kind of preparation, some thought of what he was about to do and how he was about to do it. When he went into the chapel, if only for a passing visit, he would stand for a time with his hand on the door handle before he entered the presence of his "Master and Lord," as he delighted in calling Jesus.

When we think of this example, and when we think of ourselves, and the way we run unreflectingly into prayer, and when afterward we complain that we could not pray at all, but that our minds were wandering all the time, perhaps if we cared, we could find the cause of these distractions very easily. If, before we began our prayer, we would steady our mind, withdraw it from its surroundings, and turn it in the direction along which we wish it to go, perhaps we would find a growing power of self-control. And this is especially true, and especially necessary, in any such prayer as tries to be independent of forms, such as has been here illustrated.

❧

Chapter Seven

Strive to make
your contrition perfect

A correspondent has suggested a difficulty in his prayer that is worth our consideration: He opens his prayer book. He reads the prayers before or after Confession. The words are good; he is pleased to have them and to say them; but all the time he has the suspicion that they are not his own. He comes to Confession with the weight of sin upon him. He hopes and believes that, by doing what is enjoined upon him, he will be freed from his burden. He makes his act of contrition and renews his purpose of amendment with all the earnestness of which his soul is capable. But he tells himself all the time that he has done this kind of thing before, and nothing much has come of it. And he wonders to himself whether all the time he is not soothing himself with mere words, since his resolution seems to come to so little.

In the first place, for his consolation, and for the consolation of the very many who labor under the same suspicion of themselves, let us say at once that this very attitude of mind is in itself a good sign, almost a sure sign, that all is well. In most things in life, and in prayer not least of all, it is not so much what a man can do that is his true measure, but, rather, what with all his heart he aspires to do. Human nature is surrounded with too many obstacles, is weighed down with too many burdens of all kinds, is of itself too weak and faltering to be a true gauge of the workings of that inner self which, after all, is the true man. We aspire to higher and better things. We make the effort to rise to them. By word and deed, we encourage ourselves in our endeavor. In the end, we may fail, or may seem to fail, but God has seen our heart and our effort, as well as our apparent failure, and He knows that the evil we do is not the whole story of ourselves.

In the second place this very suspicion is in itself a sure sign of progress. The man who makes an act of contrition without any thought as to whether he means it or not, who learns little of himself from repeated falls and infidelities, who trusts himself this time, as he has often done before, without much intention of greater effort, is in a far more evil plight than the man who knows his weakness and who can do little more than look up to Heaven and cry, "Lord, be merciful to me, a sinner!"[56] — yes, even though while he cries, he trembles for himself in the future.

For a perfect act of contrition, the main point is to be utterly sincere, or as sincere as we can make ourselves, at the moment that we pray. This sincerity, forcing our heart to correspond with our words, is the chief object at which we have aimed in these instructions. It may be good, then, to analyze an act of contrition in this light, in order that we may more clearly discover our own sincerity and that we may be more thorough in our contrition in the future.

For practical purposes, it may be said that an act of contrition consists of three parts, each of which is really a test of the sincerity of the other two. It contains: an acknowledgment that I have done wrong; an expression of regret that I have done it; and a determination that, because it is wrong, I will not do it again. In order that contrition may be supernatural, each of these must be referred in some way to God. Hence, they must be rewritten in some such words as the following: an acknowledgment that I have offended God; an expression

[56] Cf. Luke 18:13.

of sorrow that I have offended Him; a determination that, because this deed is an offense to Him, it shall not be done again.

It is a question of the moment when the act of contrition is made, not of the past or the future. I may have fallen often in the past, I may fall again in the future, but if, here and now, my contrition includes, sincerely, each of the three parts just mentioned, then it is true, and, what is more, in the long run it will have its effect.

As has just been said, each of these is a test and proof of the sincerity of the rest. Do I really acknowledge that what I have done is wrong? Then I shall be sorry for having done it. If I am not sorry, it is a sign that I am not quite sincere in my acknowledgment. Am I really sorry for what I have done? Then not only shall I wish I had not done it, but I shall determine that, so far as I am able, it shall not occur again. Am I really determined it shall not occur again? Then I will go back to the beginning, look and see where the wrong came in, and take means that in the future it shall be eliminated; in other words I shall determine to avoid, not only sin, but also its occasions. In this last lies the real test of our sincerity; if the determination does not reach as far as the occasions of sin, it is a sign that we are not wholehearted in our condemnation of it, and therefore our contrition is not perfect.

In order that we may be surer of the sincerity in our contrition, it will be found by experience that the deeper our motive, the truer will our contrition be. Fear, for instance, will make us repent in some measure, but it will not touch the heart of the matter. That is why we speak of sorrow built on fear as imperfect contrition. Sorrow founded on a sense of duty is better. Founded on devotion, it is better still. It is best of all when it is founded on the realization of offended Love. This is why so much depends on our attitude toward God when we make our act of contrition. If we look upon Him as merely our Judge, our contrition is of one kind. If we look upon Him as our lawful Master, it is of another. If we look upon Him as our Leader, it is yet a third. But it is best of all when we look upon Him as Love offended by what we have done — Love in Himself, Love in friendship with ourselves, Love atoning for our deeds by enduring every stab they inflict.

It may now be best to give some kind of act of contrition, not merely which shall be an act, but which shall help to secure the sinner's sincerity. I have the burden of my sin upon my conscience. I would gladly be rid of that burden. I know that God can free me from it. I know He will free me if I am sincerely sorry for my offense against Him. So I come before Him. I recall to myself who He is and who I am in comparison. I let my thoughts and affections then run on, repeating each that I may be sure that I mean them.

∾

An Act of Contrition

My God,
my Creator,
my Master,
my Friend and Lover,
my Judge,
almighty, yet all-merciful,
all angry, yet all-loving,
all just, yet all-seeing,
this evil thing I have done —
evil in itself,
evil in its degrading consequences,
evil in its offensiveness to You,
for You have forbidden it,
You detest it.

Strive to make your contrition perfect

It violates Your law, Your order.
It in some way hurts You —
I have done this thing.
I deserve the consequences.
I have no excuse.
Father, forgive me.
I have offended You,
the creature the Creator,
the slave the Master,
the beloved the Lover,
the culprit the Judge.
I deserve the consequences.
I have no excuse.
Father, forgive me.
I have offended You,
the son the Father,
the brother the Brother.
I have crucified Your Son, Jesus.
I deserve the consequences.
I have no excuse.
Father, forgive me.
I wish I had not done it,
for my own sake,
for the sake of others,

but mostly for Your sake,
for the sake of Jesus Christ.
I have hurt Him,
hurt him in His tender Heart.
It shall not happen again.
With Your help, it shall not.
Although my evil nature craves,
although my weakness fears,
I am determined,
for my own sake,
for Your sake more than mine.
I will take the means
to keep it far from me,
to avoid the danger,
to put it out of my life,
and all that leads to it.
But I am needy and poor.
O God, help me.

If you conclude with the Our Father, the Our Father itself becomes an act of perfect contrition.

Chapter Eight

❧

Beware of pietism
in yourself and others

It is sometimes said, perhaps more often it is felt, that pious people are a dreadful bore. They were "all right" until they became pious; now they are utterly unbearable. Once we could talk to them, could join them in work or in play; now they will not talk, or, if they do, the talk turns into piety that makes us stamp with rage. They will not play, or, if they do, they make us feel that it is all "out of charity" to us. We cannot even work alongside them any more than we can work alongside an iceberg or while rolling on a bed of thistles.

Nay more, and this troubles us most of all, nothing seems to make us ourselves so impious as contact with these pious people. In their absence, we were "all right" and are "all right"; the moment they come into the room, our bristles instantly rise, our tongues become sharpened, our hearts are bitter as gall, and our thoughts become unconquerable, so great is the storm that stirs them. When they are gone, it is good if we do not pursue them, or blacken the room they have left, with a torrent of abuse and contradiction that will give us endless remorse, and yet will be defended by us as just, necessary, and deserved.

There are few who have not undergone this remarkable experience. Let us own up to it and acknowledge that there are few who do not undergo it still. Yet surely the experience is remarkable. If philosophy, of every school but one, is correct, then goodness should attract, not repel, and a good man, a holy man, a pious man, should be always a treasure. How, then, are we to account for this apparent contradiction? Goodness is always attractive in theory; in practice, goodness, once it takes hold of a man, seems to make him simply repelling.

In the first place, let us be prepared to give and take. I mean, let us be prepared to own that there may be fault on both sides. The "good" man may be the intolerable bore that we think him, but it may also be that we ourselves are not wholly without blame. I once knew a man whom I thought pious and who occasionally got on my nerves. One day I discovered that he actually thought me pious, and that accounted for much. He was trying to live up to what he thought was my level, and I was giving him a very bad lead.

Or again, there may be another cause. We are told that birds of a feather flock together; we are also told that two of a trade cannot agree. Whatever may be the truth of the first of these proverbs — proverbs are never more than partial truths — it is abundantly true that too much understanding, too great intimacy, tends to make us very critical. He is a great saint indeed who, on close acquaintance, does not give some matter for complaint. And the holier one may be in some respects, the more do we exact from him in others. If no man is a hero to his valet, neither is any man a saint to his brother; for either the brother knows too much, or else his standard utterly excludes all defect.

There is yet another possibility, which may mean a fault on our side. After all, a good man among us is usually to us a constant admonition. We are holding a certain conversation. Our "pious" friend comes in, and instinctively we have to stop. He is a nuisance to us — but why? We are having a jolly time, reckless of consequences, perhaps a little reckless of duty. Our "pious" friend is seen in the offing. We shirk his company — but why? We are arguing ourselves into a course of action that our conscience all the time disavows. We consult our "pious" friend, and instead of seeing as we see, he takes the side of conscience. Such a friend is a wet blanket, a croaking pessimist, a soured misanthrope, an unsympathetic creature who will see no point of view but his own. But why this torrent of abuse? Is the fault his or ours?

These, then, are some of the lines along which, when we condemn, we may not be wholly without blame. We may be opposed to good just because it is good; and since this is against human nature, human nature invents another good that it sets itself up to defend. No saint was ever oppressed without its being shown that he was the enemy of good; no martyr was ever put to death but for apparently the best of causes; and among ourselves a good man is hardly ever judged without the soundest reasons being given. Nevertheless, it may very well be that the saint, the martyr, and even the good man have right on their side after all.

But even when all this is said, even when we have acknowledged our own possible mistakes and delinquencies, it still remains true that in very many cases, and without any reason like those above mentioned, the "pious" man is a horrid nuisance. Before his retreat, he was natural; now he is as stiff, artificial, and unbending, as only a retreat can make him. Before, he was considerate and forgiving; now he is critical and exacting, as though he had no faults of his own. Before, he kept what piety he possessed to himself; now he must forever be improving the occasion, even such as need not be improved. Worst of all — for it is the very worst — before, he did not matter much either way; now his very presence makes us bristle, his very silence makes us noisy; even in our prayers, in church or chapel, the mere consciousness that he is beside us banishes what spiritual feelings we may have cherished.

This is undoubtedly true. Undoubtedly there are pious people who do get on our nerves, even when piety alone is considered. But let us see who they are. To begin with, there are the beginners. Not all, but some are a trial, even as are most beginners of almost every kind. If they are true beginners, they are sure to be enthusiastic; and the enthusiastic, to those who are not, are always something of a trial. Again, if they are beginners, they are bound to be awkward. They are bound to overdo their part. They are bound to make mistakes. In all this, they can trouble us. Beginners, again, either ask too many questions from their eagerness to learn or else, because of their inexperience, are liable to make sweeping statements. In all this, they can offend.

But these are not half so bad as those who are older. There are some pious people on whom piety acts like starch. They seem to have taken their models from stained-glass windows, not from the saints they represent. Their ideal of spotlessness is a white marble statue, not a red human heart. Their method of devotion is ready-made, turned out by machinery; it is not made to each individual's measure. Their dealings with others are puritanical: they begin by looking for flaws, they condemn whenever they can, they yield to no one's weakness, and they judge all by standards of their own. These are the people who try us; the "unco guid," as the genial poet has called them,[57] or else the "unco dense," who cannot see other points of view than one.

I do not know whether in our hearts there are any other pious people we blame. At first, we incline to blame all, sweeping all into one condemnation. Later we discover that not all are included; some good people are also good sorts. Gradually, if we are patient, we limit very much our sentence. We begin to discover that it is

[57] Robert Burns, "Address to the Unco Guid."

not so much piety that we condemn, or that rouses us, as either piety eccentric, or piety gone mad, or piety that has frozen into pietism. Man is too true to be easily mistaken; truth recognizes truth and always loves it. If, then, there is antagonism, there will be untruth on one side or the other. But if piety is genuine, if it goes deep down and is therefore spontaneous, it is always welcome — chiefly because it is scarcely, if at all, recognized. It is blended with the character of the owner, and the character, chastened by it, dominates. Such a character we call real, and we are prepared to accept all the rest.

All this leads us to two conclusions. In the first place, let us not be in too great a hurry to condemn all piety as pietism. If we have a natural prejudice against piety and cannot account for its origin, if we have here and there met a pious individual who has gotten very much on our nerves, let us not hastily assume that all piety is annoying, that all good people are wet blankets, but let us look around and count the number of those whom we revere, not in spite of, but because of their piety.

And second, let us look to ourselves. It may be that pious people are a trouble to us, chiefly because our

Spiritual Excellence

piety is a trouble to them. We ourselves may not be immaculate in that matter. Or again, it may be that they trouble us because we do not want to be troubled. We have settled down in a comfortable little puddle of our own, and object to being disturbed. In either case, the fault may be ours. If it is, do not let piety suffer for it, even if we ourselves do not aspire so high.

Chapter Nine

Live in the present

~

Our Lord said, in His Sermon on the Mount: "Sufficient for the day is the evil thereof," and He went on to explain the practical application of His words: "Be not therefore solicitous for tomorrow; for the morrow will be solicitous for itself."[58] By this He does not encourage carelessness or want of foresight. He does not condemn thrift and prudence. He only warns us against the most common source of all our vainest anxieties: the imaginary fear of what may be. Of all the many kindnesses of God to man, is there any kindness greater than the permission to live each day as a life apart, to make of each day a perfect thing, unspoiled by what may have been, and still more by what may be? And yet is there any kindness of God more commonly neglected, more recklessly thrown away?

[58] Matt. 6:34.

Spiritual Excellence

We human beings are strange creatures. We are forever crying for the moon and neglect the solid earth on which we stand. We make nothing of that which is in our hands. Our eyes are forever wandering abroad, seeing phantoms through the mist, turning life into a nightmare, paralyzing action by the fear of that which is not. We have the present always with us, yet we are always endeavoring to live in a half-forgotten past or a fancied future. We live in the past, recalling pleasures that are no more, magnifying them out of all proportion, contrasting with them in their magnified state the trifling pleasures of today, and, by the contrast, robbing these pleasures of their meaning.

Or we look along the past and count up the mistakes we have made. We tell ourselves of all the opportunities we have lost. Our old self scolds our juvenile self for all the foolish things it has done. We weep over all that is past and gone. Even when we smile at happy recollections, it is with the smile that lingers around the mouth of a corpse.

The result of each and all is the same. We look at the present with a long, sour face. We say we have spoiled ourselves, or that our chance is over and will not return, or that evidently we are doomed to disappointment.

And beneath this self-accumulated burden we just sit down and do nothing.

Or else we live in the future. We are something at present, but it is nothing in comparison with what we may yet hope to be. We can do something today, but compared with what we might do, or yet may do, or, but for this or that interference, would do, it is not worth consideration. We peer into the darkness to discover that which we can never know. We imagine strange things that we know very well may never come to pass. We look down imaginary vistas, build our castles in the air, and fret because we are not permitted to live in them. Or, as a last perversion, if, for the moment, all is going well with us, we deliberately spoil the content-ment we might enjoy by dwelling on the time when we shall be no longer happy, or even, if we are extreme, by making ourselves miserable because we are not so.

Obviously in neither of these ways do we benefit ourselves or others, or promote our good or happiness. By both, we only wreck ourselves in the present, so far as we are able.

Looking backward has many dangers. In the first place, we easily magnify the things that are gone. We forget that in the past we were younger; and the younger we were, the greater do small things appear. Who has not experienced that sense of disappointment which often comes to one who returns to a spot after a long lapse of years? In his childhood, a person had been in some room or building. He has retained the memory of his visit. In his manhood, he visits the spot again and is oppressed with a sense of its narrowness, its puny size. So it is with much that is past. We retain the recollection, but we forget that we have grown. If time could go backward, and put us again in the circumstances after which we hanker, how narrow they would seem! How great would be our disappointment!

If this is true of past delights, how much more is it true of past miseries! Of all delusions, perhaps none is so great as the thought that our past has ruined our present, that the evils we have done, the mistakes we have committed, have made all further hope impossible. Again, for the most part, looking into the past, we repeat the mistake of the magnified room. "When I was a child," says St. Paul, "I spoke as a child, I understood as a child, I thought as a child. But when I became a man, I put away the things of a child."[59] So we, when we

[59] 1 Cor. 13:11.

were children, may indeed have done evil as children; but let us remember that it was "as children," and not as mature men and women. And so of every step after; we are always older than we were, always more mature than we were, and the resolve now, if only we will make it, is the act of a more mature creature than the evil we did yesterday. No matter who we are, if we will, it is always in our power to restore the balance.

In the same way, dreaming of the future, of what might be and what may be, has at least three paralyzing effects. It requires no great imagination to picture to ourselves some state or condition better than that which is now ours. If only this obstacle were removed, if that arrangement were made, if we ourselves were placed in such or such surroundings, how happy we would be! How much good we would be able to do! And we compare our lot with this mirage of our own making. We lose sight of the opportunities that are actually around us. We forget how much worse is the lot of many others. We ignore how little we deserve even of that which is ours. We are depressed at what we have not, neglecting that which we have. Our strength is enfeebled; our activity grows slack. We have chosen to live in dreamland, and we reap a dreamer's harvest.

Spiritual Excellence

Or there is the other side: the dwelling on imaginary fears. If we are inclined to magnify the pleasures that are past, no less do we magnify the troubles that may be before us. It is a common saying that pain in prospect is greater pain than pain that actually is upon us. Or, to put it another way, it is not so much pain as the prospect of its long continuance that will break a man down.

So it is in most other things. If only this will not happen, we shall be happy and content! We have no reason to suppose that it will, but we must worry ourselves with this shadow. If we lose this friend, we lose everything. If we lose this situation, we are doomed. If this thing goes wrong, the rest is hopeless. With these and a thousand other ifs, we shatter our moral nerve, we take the heart out of our life's work, and we render ourselves very puny things indeed.

Meanwhile the present alone is ours, and we let it slip through our fingers. The past is gone, whether for evil or for good, to be stored up in better hands than ours. The future still belongs to God alone; and it is not the least of His wonderful mercies that He keeps it entirely to Himself. It is what I am now, not what I have been or shall be, it is what I do now, not what I have done or shall do, that here and now matters most, to me, to God, and to all the world besides.

Those who face that which is actually before them, unburdened by the past, undistracted by the future, are they who live, who make the best use of their lives. These are those who have found the secret of contentment. For such, there is no day that cannot be lived through, no matter what it may bring. There is no circumstance that cannot be put to the best advantage, no matter how contrary and galling.

"Now is the acceptable time; now is the day of salvation,"[60] cried St. Paul. And he pushed on from day to day, saying every morning with the psalmist, "Now I have begun,"[61] until he discovered that his many beginnings had enabled him to fight the good fight and to complete his course.[62] To be ready for each day's duty as it comes will make us ready, when it comes, for the duty of the last day of all.

[60] 2 Cor. 6:2.
[61] Ps. 76:11.
[62] 2 Tim. 4:7.

Chapter Ten

Bear your troubles
as Jesus and Mary did

It is easy to read what St. Teresa is said to have written: "Let nothing trouble thee; let nothing annoy thee; all things pass away." It is easy for those who are at peace to preach to others the importance of not suffering themselves to be troubled. Even to ourselves, in our moments of consolation, or in our times of courage and resolution, it is easy to make up our minds that from this hour we will not let ourselves be troubled anymore.

Trouble is so opposed, peace of mind is so inculcated, by all spiritual writers that we almost come to think that there is something wrong in being troubled. And often enough, perhaps always, some of us actually measure our spiritual state by the degree of peace or of trouble that reigns within our souls.

This may be very good as a gauge to a certain extent, and with a certain class of people; but for many, perhaps for the great majority, it contains a great fallacy.

Spiritual Excellence

Without any doubt, it is a lifetime of trouble — I mean internal trouble, and not merely external difficulties — that has been the salvation and perfection of many. For some, it may even be said that the endurance of trouble, the groping through black darkness, the endurance of irritation, the feeling about anxiously in the midst of confusion, doubt, and temptation, the depression that comes of the inner sense of failure in things, whether spiritual or temporal — the endurance of trouble in these or other shapes is a characteristic feature of sanctity.

We can go even further. Twice at least in Scripture is it expressly told us of our Lady that she was troubled, and on other occasions it is more than implied. Indeed, we may say that her whole life seems scarcely intelligible unless we assume a certain jarring element of trouble running through it all. Of her Son, our Lord Jesus Christ, it is still more emphatically true. Five times at least we find Him described to us as distinctly troubled; not merely feeling things — for that kind of trouble was seldom absent from Him — and not merely enduring annoyance — which, as He said, was His accepted lot — but emphatically, as we should say, disturbed in mind because of something that had happened. In trouble, then, as in everything else, these two have given us an example, have come right down to our level.

Can we discover from their troubles anything for ourselves? Can we draw any conclusion that will guide us in the troubles that come upon us, especially as to those which we might learn to bear, and those which, even though they crush us, are still consistent with sanctity?

Let us take first the troubles of our Lord. There is the trouble that came on Him as He stood over the tomb of Lazarus. "Jesus, therefore," says St. John the Evangelist, par excellence, of the troubles of our Lord, "when He saw her [Mary] weeping, and the Jews that were come with her weeping, groaned in the spirit, and troubled Himself."[63] He is troubled at the trouble of those around Him. His sympathy for them makes Him "groan in the spirit." He is troubled at the loss of a friend, even though He knows that He is going to bring him back to life. Even so, in a memorable sermon, do we see the sweet soul of St. Bernard[64] break down and sob at the loss of a friend; and when again he finds his words, he is unable

[63] John 11:33.
[64] St. Bernard (1090-1153), Abbot of Clairvaux.

to continue his discourse, but must proclaim the praises of the friend he has lost.

Next our Lord is troubled in the midst of the procession on Palm Sunday. "And when He drew near," says St. Luke, "seeing the city, He wept over it."[65] And the reason immediately follows. He is troubled because He has been rejected, not on His own account — He is not indignant, He is not offended; He says nothing of insult or honor — but because of the woes that He sees will come to those who will not receive Him. So is a priest or a teacher often troubled when he sees a soul deliberately walking to his doom. So are a father and a mother sometimes troubled because a wayward son or daughter will have his or her way and will pay no heed to those who know better. Such trouble, such heart-eating trouble, is consistent with the highest sanctity.

The third occasion is that on which our Lord describes Himself as troubled, and it is one full of mystery. Some Gentiles had come for a festival. They asked that they might be introduced to Jesus. An apostle spoke for them, and He answered with a few words in the middle of which these occur: "Now is my soul troubled. And

[65] Luke 19:41.

what shall I say: 'Father, save me from this hour'? But for this cause I came into this hour. Father, glorify Thy name."[66] What, here, can the cause of His trouble be? Is it not that which everyone must feel who sees the number of those who have not yet known the name of God and His Christ? So was St. Paul continually troubled; so St. Francis Xavier in the midst of the Eastern heathen; so the many saints who have burned with zeal for the house of God and have spent themselves on its account.

Again, early in the course of the Last Supper, our Lord is troubled. After He had washed the feet of His disciples and had spoken of the example He had given, St. John says of Him, "When Jesus had said these things, He was troubled in spirit; and He said, 'Amen, amen, I say to you, one of you shall betray me.' "[67] Surely a legitimate trouble is this, whether we consider the treachery of the friend or the consequences to the traitor. And let us not make too much of the second of these alternatives; that the first ate into the soul of our Lord is clearly evidenced from His words spoken to the traitor in the garden: "Friend, whereto art thou come? Judas, dost

---

[66] John 12:27-28.
[67] John 13:21.

thou betray the Son of Man?"[68] Treachery must always
give trouble, even though we may have the courage at
the same time to "rejoice that we are accounted worthy
to suffer for the name of Jesus";[69] but the treachery of a
friend is the cruelest of all.

Lastly, there is the hour of greatest trouble, which
preceded and culminated in the Agony in the Garden.
The Evangelists vie with each other in looking for
words by which to express it. "He began to grow sorrowful and to be sad," says one.[70] "He began to fear and to be
heavy," says another.[71] "Being in an agony, he prayed
the longer," says the third;[72] and all record His words:
"My soul is sorrowful even unto death."[73] Nor do these
English words convey the full sense of amazement and
depression that is contained in the Greek original. He is
so troubled that He seems to be unable to help Himself.
He seeks support from others — from His disciples, and

[68] Matt. 26:50; Luke 22:48.

[69] Acts 5:41.

[70] Matt. 26:37.

[71] Mark 14:33.

[72] Luke 22:43.

[73] Matt. 26:38; Mark 14:34.

they fail Him; from His Father, and at first it seems to be long in coming; from an angel, who does not remove the trouble, but brings Him the support He needs.

And why is He so troubled? Because of "the chalice," whatever that may mean. We cannot hope to know all, but we can draw out a few ingredients. He was troubled because He had been, and yet would be, rejected. He was troubled because He loved so much those who had rejected Him. Perhaps most of all, He was weighed down by the burden of their sins, which He had taken upon Himself as though they were His own.

So has the burden of the evil-doing of mankind oppressed the hearts and souls of men who have recognized it: the popes in all ages, the saints whose lot it has been to rule, the weary priest in our crowded cities, all, we may say, who have been given the care of others. Of all the troubles of man, perhaps none more conduces to indignation; perhaps there is none that tempts us more to steel our hearts and to leave man to his self-inflicted doom. Yet when the temptation is upon us, it is good to remember that just this trouble, harrowing as it is, death-dealing to our own spiritual peace of mind as it is, nevertheless brings us nearer to our Lord in His worst moments than does any other prayer or sacrifice.

Now let us put alongside these the two expressed troubles of our Lady. First is that which she felt at the Annunciation. When the angel had come in and had saluted her with his greeting: "Hail, full of grace. The Lord is with thee; blessed art thou among women," the Evangelist adds that Mary "having heard, was troubled at his saying, and thought within herself what manner of salutation this should be."[74] She was troubled, but not in doubt, as was Zachary on a like occasion.[75] She was troubled because, as is said of her several times afterward, "she did not understand." There was something new, something of a revolution in all this; she did not know to what it pointed; the will of God for her had become confused. So have the greatest saints been troubled at moments of crisis in their lives. So, for example, was St. Teresa often troubled. So is many a soul troubled who seeks earnestly to find that will and is suffered to remain in the dark.

The next occasion is far more easily understood. Our Lady had lost her Son. She had looked for Him for three long days. When she found Him, the trouble of her

[74] Luke 1:28-29.
[75] Luke 1:20.

heart would not contain itself. "Son, why hast Thou done so to us?" she said. "Behold Thy father and I have sought thee sorrowing."[76] This is a trouble that needs no parallel. Whatever commentators may say as to the possible self-accusation in our Lady's heart, the simple fact is quite enough: she had lost Him — *she, Him* — and only an odd person can fail to understand the implications of this loss. But perhaps there are some who understand it more than others; not merely good mothers who have been forced to part with a child they have loved, but those who at some time in their lives have been permitted to draw very near to their Lord and then seemed to have lost Him. How many of this kind have cried, "Why hast Thou done so to us?" and have been told that it was because of "His Father's business"![77] Let such remember the troubled heart of our Lady.

We are not told of other troubles of hers, even at times when it might have been expected. We are not told that she was troubled at the birth of her Child in poverty and want, or at the painful prophecy of Simeon, or because they were cruelly driven into exile, or when

[76] Luke 2:48.
[77] Luke 2:49.

she wished to see her Son and apparently could not see Him, or even when she stood beneath His Cross and watched Him bleed slowly to death. That there was trouble we know, but we are not told of it. All we see is the quiet, enduring Mother, "keeping these things, and pondering them in her heart,"[78] the model of many a silent, suffering woman who sees, and feels, and says nothing while her heart within her is breaking. Here, then, again we have an aspect of trouble that many of us can appreciate.

From these examples, we can safely conclude that a troubled heart is not always a heart that is faltering or faithless. There are troubles from without and troubles from within that are consistent with perfection. To kill the power of feeling these troubles, to put ourselves, in this sense, beyond the reach of trouble, may be very good philosophy — let philosophers look to that! — but it is no special imitation of our Lord and His Mother. To be troubled at the loss of a friend is possible for a saint; to be above such trouble means, if anything, something on the other side. It is good to be troubled when the will of God is not done among men. It is good to be troubled at

[78] Luke 2:51.

the failure of those who are clearly called to high emprises. It is consistent to be troubled when God leaves us, as He does at times, wholly in the dark. In these and in many other ways, trouble may come to a faithful soul.

But there are many other troubles that we can well afford to lay aside. What are they? Their number is legion, and we shall know what they are as they come to us, if only we will cling to Him who is the Prince of Peace. It was of these that He spoke when He said, "Let not your heart be troubled, nor let it be afraid. You believe in God, believe also in me."[79] And it was to those who were troubled in this way that He cried, "Come to me, all you that labor and are burdened, and I will refresh you. Take up my yoke upon you, and learn of me, because I am meek and humble of heart; and you shall find rest for your souls. For my yoke is sweet and my burden light."[80] Our Lord was troubled in the garden, but we are not told that He was troubled at the sight of the Cross.

[79] John 14:1.
[80] Matt. 11:28-30.

Chapter Eleven

∽

Turn to Christ
as your truest friend

What do I mean by a friend? I mean something that is almost too much to be looked for in this world. I mean one whose nature is so large that it will understand and sympathize with all my myriad varied moods. I mean a man who, when he finds me mean and groveling, will not despise me; when he sees me harsh and critical, will not condemn my hardness of heart; when I am cruel in judgment, in word or in action, will bear with me until I recover my senses; when I am proud, high-handed, vain, or inflated with myself, will smile and endure, knowing that this is only a passing whim; when I am ill-tempered, peevish, or melancholy, will pity me and wait until the disease has run its course and the color of health has returned.

I mean by a friend one who will give as well as take. I mean one who, when he, in turn, is in trouble, will not hide it from me. I mean one who will not give me the

everlasting feeling that the weakness is all mine, while
he is in possession of unending peace and calm. I mean
one who will trust me far enough to let me see his weakness as I let him see mine, knowing that I, too, will not
misunderstand, or misinterpret, or become impatient,
or condemn, or turn upon my heel and walk no more
with him, even as I know he will not do to me.

This is the other side of friendship, harder to discover than the first, yet if one would be my friend, in the
deep sense in which I understand it, he must give me
this as I give the same to him. He must trust me thus far,
even as I trust him. If he is only my patron, my protec-
tor, my guide, my model, or my ideal, he may be very
much deserving of love and honor, but he is not strictly
my friend.

I mean by a friend one with whom there are no dif-
ferences. Whatever our respective gifts of nature and of
grace may be, it must be all the same between him and
me. If he thinks me clever, or learned, or strong, or even
holy, he will neither bow before me, nor treat me as a
being of another grade. Although I may know him to
have rank, wealth, athletic skill, or wit, these things,
when I think of him, will scarcely enter my mind. We
take each other for granted, without suspicion, without

reserve, without doubt. The rest are mere appendages, belonging to one as much as to the other, affecting so little our equality that we never give them a thought.

Such is what I mean by a friend. So perfect a union is friendship. But where is such a friend? Am I asking too much of human nature? Is a relation so perfect possible in this life? I wonder.

The young soul sets out on his journey and hopes to find such a comrade on his way. He takes hold of first one and then another, telling himself that he has found what he needs, but how often has he been disappointed! First, he gave his friendship to one older than himself and soon discovered he had a patron, not a friend; good, true, loyal, sound, but not what he meant by a friend. This first would-be friend, for all that the longing soul gave, showed but one side in return; he was too good, too loyal, too sound — let us say it — to be wholly true. He had the strength to guide, the virtue to endure; he lacked the humility that is essential to the ideal of friendship.

This has been the most common disappointment of my life: that hardening of friendship into mere patronage, that murder of friendship because my friend would not let me see him as he was. I gave him all. He gave me back only my reflection; himself he hid behind the mirror. I say nothing of false friends or of shallow friends. These are incapable of friendship; and to have found them out, to have fathomed all their possibilities, to have weighed them in the balance and found them wanting, is no disappointment. It is a growth in the knowledge of mankind. Disappointment comes only when one has proven and knows the possibility of friendship, and, behold, it has frozen in the making.

Yet there have been satisfactions. There have been moments when, as it were, in spite of itself, friendship has broken through the mist and glimmered golden. An old man, a superior of mine, once, in a moment of great trouble, came for refuge to my room and there burst into tears. That was a moment of happy agony, a moment of perfect friendship.

Once, in a crowd of great men and ladies, where I was but a mechanical official, there passed me by a man who had been a schoolfellow, whom I had not seen since school days, and that was years ago. He saw me; I saw him. Not a word passed between us. I have never seen him since, yet that moment was a moment of perfect friendship. More I will not say by way of illustration, lest friendship itself resent this public avowal.

Turn to Christ as your truest friend

Yes, friendship, even of the kind that is here meant, is possible in its degree, for man's nature is beyond fathoming; his capabilities of love are only short of infinite. Still, it is only in its degree. Even from the best of human friends I must not ask more than he can give. For think of all it calls for. It calls for a mind that can understand another mind without need of words. It calls for a heart that can bleed more from sympathy and fellow-feeling than from any suffering of its own. It calls for a soul so holy, so humble in its holiness, that it will give its all, its worst as well as its best, uncovered and undisguised into the hands of its friend. It calls for a will that can go to all lengths, asking no questions, making no conditions, when the question of friendship demands it.

"Who is weak and I am not weak? Who is scandalized and I am not on fire?"[81] "Greater love than this no man hath, that he lay down his life for his friend."[82] Where is all this to be found, united in any one human being? Where indeed!

Insist on the last drop of blood, and you will find it only in One. There is no human friendship that cannot

[81] 2 Cor. 11:29.
[82] John 15:13.

be snapped, that cannot be tried beyond its strength, even though it means the death of one or the other. In One only is it invincible. One mind alone understands, better far than I understand myself, and has understood from the beginning, without any need of words of mine to tell it. One heart has bled, first from its own crushing, but more because of the crushing of my heart, and bleeds on still, the more when my own has ceased to do so. One soul has made itself in all things like to mine, has shown me all it has and all it is, its strength and its seeming weakness, its gladness and its broken part, its temptations, its indignation, its tears, its appeals for help, its cries of pain, distress, and desolation. One will alone has refused to set limits alike to its giving and to its receiving, has asked for no terms, has made no stipulations, has found me as I am, and has become one with me, my good and my evil, my weakness and my strength, without a word, without a thought of what it set aside for my sake. One alone has not only borne my sorrows and carried my griefs, but has shown me His own, has "become sin"[83] for me, has made Himself one with me and taken all the consequences; and yet withal, remains

[83] Cf. 2 Cor. 5:21.

unexhausted. There is still no cry that He has given enough, that He can descend no lower, that He declines to show me — even me — every side of His nature.

So, have I not reason to be contented? I show Him all my failures and my troubles, knowing that He does not merely listen, pity, and patronize, but gives me of His own and lets me see His wounds and His weakness in return. I bring Him all my strength, my little doughty deeds of which I am so childishly proud, and I know He does not make too much of my vainglory; much less does He make too much of me. Instead, He rejoices with me when I rejoice, weeps with me when I weep, but then, and most of all, swallows up my rejoicing and weeping in His own.

Yes, even on earth, I have found a perfect friend. "I have found Him whom my soul loveth; I have held Him and will not let Him go."[84] "From all others, willy nilly, you must someday be torn apart. Love Him and keep Him for your friend, who, when all else secedes, will not leave you, nor suffer you to perish in the end!"[85]

---

[84] Cant. 3:4 (RSV = Song of Sol. 3:4).

[85] Thomas à Kempis, *Imitation of Christ*, Bk. 2, ch. 7, no. 2.

Chapter Twelve

❧

*Strive to see
goodness in others*

It does not require much insight or philosophy to discover that, in spite of much that appears on the surface, and in spite of endless warnings and gruesome pictures, human nature is not wholly evil.

Nay more, we can without much fear go further and say that no human being was yet made who was wholly evil. Shakespeare tried to create one, but he acknowledged in the end that the being he had created was not human. Dickens tried several times over, but he did so only by omitting the human element in every case. The more fiendish his characters, the less are they drawn from life.

In some human beings, it is true, the good that is in them may be much covered over. In others, it may have had little opportunity for development. In others, again, it may be of a nature so little akin to the good that is in us that we almost call it something else. Yet others may have so preponderating a balance of evil in their composition that the good may be utterly eclipsed.

Nonetheless it is there somewhere. Human nature being what it is, we cannot doubt that it is never wholly evil; that belongs to the Devil only, and even of the Devil there are points of view that leave us mystified. At all events, I do not know a description of a devil in literature that does not leave us with some sense of sympathy. Milton's devils are admirable; Dante's devils stir our pity; Goethe's devil makes us feel what a good thing has been wasted. Human nature seems incapable of imagining that which is wholly bad, just because it is not wholly bad itself.

It follows from this that a man can, if he likes, always have a kindly feeling for his fellowman, no matter what may be the provocation to the contrary. Indeed, he has a duty to do so; and the greater he is, the less will he be influenced by a single point of view and the more will he endeavor to see all around and upon the whole conception to pass his judgment.

Let us, then, in our dealings with others, remind ourselves of one or two principles, quite platitudinous in themselves, but which, nevertheless, if we will keep them in mind, will save us many a rash judgment, and harsh word, and hasty action. For such things are the characteristics of small people. When we ourselves are guilty of them, we know how puny and despicable we are in our own eyes and in those of others. Moreover, they cultivate puniness and react upon their perpetrators in a multitude of ways.

The first principle is to accept what has already been said — that is, to believe in everybody. Let us call it the principle of faith. There are some who preach the opposite; they say the prudent man will believe in nobody. But the doctrine of such people condemns itself, for it forbids us to believe in them. If they merely said, "Put implicit faith in nobody," they might have a case, for there is no one who has not a weak point somewhere, on which, for his sake as well as for our own, it is unfair to put too much reliance.

But there is a world of difference between putting an implicit trust in others and believing in them. The former may be, and more often than not is, an act of weakness, a mere leaning for self-support, an endeavor to shift our own responsibility to the shoulders of another. The latter is the deliberate act of a strong man and is usually a support and strengthening to others even more than to ourselves.

Spiritual Excellence

By believing in others, then, we mean the conviction that the evil a bad man may do does not represent the whole man; that the failure of a man does not show all his capabilities; that whatever may be a man's weakness, it is usually only a covering for something very strong and beautiful underneath. We may pass by unnoticed a quiet, harmless, passive creature and ignore him with the pitying comment that he has nothing in him; but we may also be ignoring as deep a soul as we shall ever meet in our lifetime. We may set aside a man because he is a miserable failure; but we may be also trampling on a throbbing, bleeding heart, whose yearnings are far greater than our own, which feels its failures greater than do we, which has failed while we have succeeded chiefly because its ideals are greater than ours.

Or again, we may be roused to indignation against some confirmed criminal, some utterly bad man. But we may not know that the same poor creature is equally disgusted and indignant with himself; that it is his circumstances more than himself that stand responsible for his condition; that if we had had his chances and no more, our fate would have been a poor thing; that, even as it is, his outlook is such as would make us happier creatures

envious; that, for all his wickedness, there are nevertheless those who know him better than we, and understand him better than we, and have an unaccountable
attraction and affection for something he possesses.
Even *Oliver Twist*'s Bill Sykes was loved by Nancy —
and by his dog. And to be loved with sincerity by one
who knows us implies something in us that is lovable.
Who that has dealt much with criminals has not felt
this lovableness peering out in all sorts of places?

The second principle is that of hope, and this means
that we should be confident that no good deed we ever
do is wasted. It is true we may fail in our immediate object; we may not always gain the good effect we in-
tended. We may work for a conversion, and our friend
may die without any sign of having once ever given the
matter a thought. We may give an alms and find we
have only been encouraging a wastrel. We may labor to
exhaustion in teaching a child, and the child may turn
out nothing but a shame to his instructors.

Still, none of these covers the whole matter. A good
deed done is like a stone that is dropped in deep water;
the circles of waves continue to move out from that
center, on and on, long after the stone has settled at the
bottom.

Spiritual Excellence

Let us examine these cases in some detail. I teach a child and seem to myself to have failed, to have wasted my time and energy. But others do not see it in the same light. The child himself does not. Others have been stimulated by that which I have done, in ways and to efforts altogether out of my ken. The child himself has a memory stored away in his heart, which someday will lead to his repentance. And besides these waves of blessing that have been started, with results more far-reaching than any dream of mine would have fancied, there is the lasting good done to myself; there is the fulfillment of a noble duty to mankind; there is the glory of a sacrifice given to God; there is the likeness to Jesus Christ, then most of all when my effort is least rewarded. And none of these may be neglected in the reckoning.

So again with a wasted alms. I may not approve of indiscriminate almsgiving, but that does not prevent me from seeing that even indiscriminate almsgiving is not wholly bad. Nine times out of ten, I may be cheated, but if the tenth time I failed, in a case of real distress, could I ever forgive myself? And besides, it is not every wastrel who is wholly reprobate; even among beggars there have been saints. The wastrel who meets you may not deserve your penny. If he receives it, he may even chuckle at his fortune, and your weakness. Nevertheless, as often as not, he goes away with something more than a penny in his hand, something in his heart of which he is not aware, but which someday will bear fruit: the memory of one who has treated him above that which he has deserved, the memory of a kind deed done.

Talk someday, if you like, with any common vagrant. Get his confidence and see what he will have to say, not with the object of deceiving you, but on a footing of equality. A hundred to one, he will harp upon one or two subjects: the kindness he has received from someone in a moment of particular crisis, or the wish — perhaps I should call it despair — lying at the back of his heart that he could have been or could be different. He may make no change in his life after he has spoken; he may show his deliberate intention to make no change; he may spend your alms at the nearest alehouse. But he will probably add your memory to that of others who did not treat him wholly as a pariah, who for a moment let him feel that, in spite of all, he was a man among men. Perhaps some of us would not think that in such a case our alms was wholly wasted.

Spiritual Excellence

Similarly, we might argue about that still more hopeless matter: the conversion of one dear to us — more hopeless in one sense, because the special end we have in view seems so seldom to be gained, but surely not more hopeless when we think of the supernatural forces with which we are venturing to deal. Here more than anywhere else, we have the guarantee of God Himself that our efforts are not in vain, and in those safe hands we are content to trust our all.

The third principle is that of charity, which means that we should take a chance of doing good when we get it, and should not be too often on our own defensive. Charity does not calculate too much. Charity is not too discriminating. Charity does not care to haggle. Charity does not demand a *quid pro quo*. Charity expects to make many a mistake. Charity shuts its eyes and goes on.

This is a point that needs little development; it only needs that we should take it to ourselves — prudently and wisely, if we like, but nonetheless truly and practically. We can always see the beauty of self-sacrificing charity in others. Let us not forget that in ourselves it can be no less beautiful. In others, we can see its conquering power; the same can it effect in us.

Strive to see goodness in others

"There remain, then," to use the words of St. Paul, "these three."[86] Faith teaches us to believe in everybody, not as satisfied optimists, but as men among our fellow-men. Hope gives us the confidence that nothing we do is wasted. Charity goes further; it bids us not easily to miss a chance of doing good, not to act on the defensive, never to use the argument that we are not obliged as a reason for standing aloof.

You want to do something worth doing before you die; seize the opportunities that are given to you every day, and in the end you will find that something has been done. Do not be forever waiting for the great occasion and fretting because it never seems to come. If you keep waiting, and meanwhile do nothing, either the occasion will never come, or when it comes, you will not recognize it, or you will be so utterly unpracticed in the art of doing and giving that you will be unable to seize it.

On the contrary, make your own occasion. Give, and give, and give again. You will find that one great deed will lead to another; your hands will never be empty. There is always work for such workers; this is a

[86] 1 Cor. 13:13.

profession that is not overstocked, in which competition is not great, yet whose profits are portentous.

Of what kind are those profits? Not always of money, although even in the matter of money, it is strange how often genuine charity is requited, but rather of blood; not of broad acres, but of human hearts; not perhaps in the goods of this world, which rust and the worm destroy, but in a world where there are no thieves, and canker does not enter.[87]

[87] Cf. Matt. 6:19-20.

Chapter Thirteen

❧

Base your view
of others on truth

When we are young, we naturally believe in everyone we meet. A child who has had anything like a home has been brought up on trust and confidence. He has not learned to disbelieve or doubt, at all events those whom he knows.

Still, even a child instinctively fears those he does not know; a stranger is to him something to be dreaded, something to be suspected of being on the whole more evil than good.

When we grow a little older, we think we outgrow this fear. But in fact, it is commonly more intensified, although it may show itself along another line. Some may call it shyness; some may call it criticism. Whatever outward expression it may assume, there is a tendency in us to think hard things of those whom we do not know, to picture strangers to ourselves as persons to be feared rather than welcomed, to dread meeting them, and to be anxious even to pain about what we shall find when we make their acquaintance.

When the meeting does come, in nine cases out of ten, we are agreeably surprised. The stranger is very much like us. The great man is not so great; or if he is, he is obviously great against his will. The scholar is a child, the soldier a schoolboy magnified. We come across them one by one and condemn ourselves for our preconceived judgments. When we made them, we were little better than children; we feared what was unknown. When we come to know it, we are ashamed of our fears.

From this it is safe to make a general conclusion, and it is this: Most men are better than the estimate we form of them before we know them. Our first judgments, founded on hearsay, or on some wholly alien evidence, must necessarily be exaggerated. It is deprived of the means of filling in the lights and the shades that personal contact alone can provide. If we hear of another's talents, we magnify the poor victim in our minds until he becomes a perfect monster. If we are told of his strength of will, we imagine some inhuman cyclops. If we have proof of his fascinating personality, we picture some siren of the sea that will lure us, unless we are careful, to our destruction.

Then comes the discovery, and with it often the reaction to the opposite extreme. Monster as the creature
of our imagination was, it was nevertheless an idol; we
meet the man in real life and find him only human. So,
very often, our second judgments are as unsound as our
first. Our monster falls so short of our anticipation that
we declare him to be overrated, forgetting that it is we
alone who have done him this injustice. Our strong
man never seems to put forth his strength, and we wonder whether he really has any. And so with all the rest of
the idols that our fancy has set up.

But if this is true of every type of man, it is particu-
larly true of those who earn that most unenviable of rep-
utations: the reputation for being good. Poor creatures!
What a time such people have! A man is talked about as
being holy. He has had the misfortune to utter some
spiritual remark. He has been seen to do or not to do
something that has been taken as proving his mortified
spirit. He has been found somewhere on his knees —
perhaps asleep — and the word has gone round that he
is a man of prayer. We hear of him and are curious. We
wonder whether, after all, he is going to come across a
live saint; whether there will be a halo around his head,
whether his hands will have wounds in them, whether

his haggard face will bear the marks of long fasting, whether at the very least his eyes will be forever closed or else forever turned upward so that the white alone will appear.

Then comes the meeting. There is no halo; perhaps there is instead a rather unruly head of hair. There are no wounds; instead there is a daintiness, almost a fop-pishness about his fingers that is worthy of a dandy. He has scarcely a wrinkle on his face; on the contrary, he is quite aggressively healthy looking, with not a shade of mortification. His eyes are not cast down, much less are they turned up; rather, they twinkle at a joke, look around at everything of interest, and almost make you think of the warning that the eyes are the windows of the soul. And as for his conversation — well, really! He asks how you are. He talks about the weather. He re-marks on the news in the morning paper. He discusses some triviality suggested by a book on the table or a pic-ture on the wall. He propounds just the same common-place platitudes that everybody else drones out. His behavior is no less disappointing — so uneven, so given to long silence or else to rather inordinate laughter, so easygoing, so ordinary, perhaps even, if we watch him closely, not always in very good taste.

And this is your saint! We forget that it is we who are to blame. We had no business to divorce our ideal from human nature. In our picture, we have eliminated a saint's first characteristic: his hiddenness. But besides, and perhaps worse, we have taken the remarks of others and magnified them so that those who uttered them could never have recognized the original. They never said he was a saint; they merely said he was a true human being who suited their fancy. They never said he was mortified; they merely said he did not always take sugar in his tea. They never said he was a man of prayer; they merely found him once fingering his beads. We have added the rest, and the poor man gets a bad time of it at our hands.

When, then, we make up our minds about a person, let us give both ourselves and our victim a fair start. The chances are that every man we meet is a human being and not a portent; and every human being has his weaknesses as well as his good points. No one is wholly bad; very few are wholly good.

If, then, we hear anyone indiscriminately praised, let us not at once imagine to ourselves an ideal so perfect that we must inevitably be disappointed when we meet him. Nor, on the other hand, need we, because of our disappointment, cancel all that we have heard. Probably the truth lies midway between the two. If the man is not the unrivaled genius we fancied, he may be very talented all the same. If he does not always show his power, it may be there ready for its occasion. If he is not a saint, he may have that in him which makes for sanctity. Few people do not say a good thing sometimes. Few are not mortified in some respects. Even if there are few who pray, at least there are few who do not desire it and who do not make the effort sometimes. Or to put our conclusion another way, if we did not form our judgments of others beforehand, we would usually find that our impressions of them would almost invariably be good.

There is another factor that may often warp our estimate of others. The story is told in various forms of the visitor who was being shown through a mental hospital by a harmless inmate, sensible on every point but one. As they walked along a corridor, they passed another inmate. "See that man," said the guide, "what do you think is his craze? He actually thinks himself to be the Holy Spirit!" Then, as the visitor made no comment, he added, "Isn't he absurd, considering I am the Holy Spirit myself?"

Base your view of others on truth

Now, how many of us have a touch of this lunacy in ourselves? How many of us have not noticed that if we fancy ourselves in any way, if we think ourselves rather clever, or strong-willed, or brilliant, or pious, we are inclined to be hard on those who have a reputation for the same? We do not like to own it; we are ashamed of ourselves when we discover it; but there is no more sure proof of vanity than the refusal to brook another star of our particular magnitude in our own horizon. Nor, we may add, is there any more sure proof that we are not that which we imagine ourselves to be.

Mere intellectual brilliance resents a rival, but a really clever man welcomes the ability of another. Sham strength fears competition, but a really strong man rejoices in the strength of a companion. Imitation sanctity must shine alone, but a really holy man has no greater satisfaction than the discovery and promotion of another's holiness.

It is often said that the perfection of good manners consists in being perfectly natural and perfectly true. This explains why, in the opinion of very many, the contented poor are often the best-mannered people in the world. Whether the statement is true or not, a very little modification makes it safe. Good manners are

Spiritual Excellence

founded on a certain give-and-take. If we are ourselves, neither more nor less, if we take others for what they are, neither less nor more, if we adapt ourselves to them, and them to ourselves, without any presumption or arrogance, then we shall behave as we should. This is the life that is true, in the exterior as well as within. And this is why, when we meet a saint, if we ever do, we shall be most struck, not by his sanctity, nor by his abstraction, but by the yielding deference of his manners. He appreciates the good he finds in others; he shows that good its due respect. And the consequent behavior is one of those links that inseparably unite the saint with all mankind.

Chapter Fourteen

⌒

Pray for the return
of those who have fallen
away from the Faith

∽

"Who is weak, and I am not weak? Who is scandalized, and I am not on fire?"[88]

There are many sufferings in life — I mean, many veins of suffering, along which pain wells from the human heart and back to it. But there is one agony distinct from all the rest, which, when felt, gives us a totally new idea of the suffering of the Heart of Christ, our Lord. It is the suffering, the peculiar agonizing void, the torture that makes moaning no relief, nor motion of the body any change, which we feel when we watch a soul we dearly love deliberately exchanging good for evil.

A soul comes across our path. In a very little time, we see him to be transparent as crystal, a thing of real beauty, all the more beautiful because he does not know it himself. We revel in the sunshine of his presence. The

[88] 2 Cor. 11:29.

thought of evil is banished when he is there. At the sight of him, at the thought of him, we thank God that He has made man. Delicate and perfect he has grown up out of and amid the evil that lies wallowing around him, and by his mere presence there, we know that all the rest is worthwhile.

One day we are puzzled. We can point to nothing in particular; we can lay our hands on nothing. The glittering eye is there; the artless confidence of action is there; even the happy laugh, and frank expression, and merry overflow of words. And yet through and around it all, there is something that we cannot detect, which was not there before. So thin is the film covering it that we blame ourselves for rash judgment. We tell ourselves that it is at most only a new phase of the soul to which our eyes have not yet been accustomed.

Nevertheless, it is there, and remains, and soon finds a clearer definition. The laughing eye still laughs, but perhaps with a certain conscious boldness. The artless confidence of action has something aggressive in it. The frankness is too dramatic, the language too loud. There is an exaggeration somewhere that does not ring true. And once that jarring is discovered, then begin in the chords of our heart a sympathetic jarring, a wondering at it knows not what, an aching that will not be located, a wandering of mind, an aimlessness of action, a reaching out to any kind of relief, a yearning to do something where there is nothing to be done, a craving to shed tears that will not come — all these are the signs of the storm that is about to burst.

Then comes the revelation. It will be in some gesture, some strange accidental word, some attitude of thought expressed in an idle manner that will reveal the terrible truth to the soul who loves. Things are not what they were. The rose has gotten a cankerworm. The word has been uttered, the allusion has been made, the deed has been done that has opened the understanding eyes of one to whom the poor child is dear, and henceforth it seems that there can be no rest for him again.

No, there is no greater agony in human life than to be compelled to watch a human soul deliberately turning to evil before our very eyes — above all, a soul who has already grown long in innocence. The agony has been too much for many before today. It has driven them to murder or to suicide, or both. They would rather see their child dead at their feet but innocent, than living but beginning to corrupt. They would rather die themselves than live and endure the sight of the robbery of this treasure of their soul. The reckless child laughs at the agony he causes. He refuses to see the harm that is done. He claims his rights. He rests upon his own strength. He turns with indignation against any word of remonstrance. He will do what he likes, and no one shall interfere. He knows his own mind and needs no warning. He takes one step cautiously at first; he takes a second more coolly; with the third he gets his stride; the fourth begins to run and pierces the heart that loves and sees and understands and knows only too well the inevitable end of that career.

In truth, we reckless creatures seldom consider what we are doing when we play fast and loose with right and wrong. We know we make ourselves miserable by it, but we pretend not to care about that. We do not always know how miserable we make others, or, if we do, we affect not to believe it. But often enough, for the sake of someone else, we will avoid evil, even when we will not avoid it for our own. And if we would only realize how our own determination hurts the heart of one we love, perhaps we would at least think twice before we acted.

I do not know what good can come of needlessly hurting others. I do not even know what self-satisfaction the most selfish human being can gain by it. Yet I do know that many a time in life a person who is going from good to bad, or from bad to worse, will trample on the hearts of those who love him — a mother's, a father's, a sister's, a brother's, a husband's, a wife's, a truly loving friend's — reveling in the blood that is spilled, even while each stamp of the foot sends agony into his own heart, and, when asked why he so acts, he will cry out simply that he chooses to do so. It is the hardest thing to understand in human life, this deliberate defiance of common human feeling by the person who determines to have his own way. It is the most fruitful cause of misery in every home. Yet it is found again and again, and the cause is always the same.

But sometimes there comes an awakening, and then how the tables are turned! The person who did the harm is affected for the rest of his life, either with remorse or with contrition. He sees what he has done, to himself and to others. He sees what others have done to him and for him, and what they are ever willing to do. And the discovery is terrible indeed. If there were tears before, hard, bitter tears of self-will, now there are tears, many more, from the heart, and not only from the eyes.

171

Spiritual Excellence

But they are tears that make others thank God. "Peter, going out, wept bitterly,"[89] but Christ, our Lord, rejoiced at the tears that were shed. And so it is often with us. The time may be long, the way may be stony, the agony may drag along, but if we will leave the ninety-nine alone, and go after the strayed one until we find it,[90] please God it will be there at last. And when it is found to be there, it is also found to have been worthwhile — worth all the suffering, the sleeplessness and long-dragging days, although not worth the bitterness of the poor thing who insisted on having his way. "And when he hath found it, doth he not lay it upon his shoulders, rejoicing; and coming home, calleth together his friends and neighbors, saying to them, 'Rejoice with me, because I have found my sheep that was lost'? I say to you that even so there shall be joy in Heaven upon one sinner that doth penance, more than upon ninety-nine just who need not penance."[91]

---

[89] Cf. Matt. 26:75.
[90] Cf. Luke 15:4.
[91] Luke 15:5-7.

Chapter Fifteen

*Learn to benefit
from your falls*

If to look on and watch a beautiful soul deteriorating before our eyes is an agony almost intolerable, if such an agony leaves behind it a scar upon the heart that nothing can ever quite heal, no less is the internal grief of the deteriorating soul itself a thing terrible to witness. In some degree, we have all felt it — that grief which conscience inflicts on us when we have done something utterly unworthy.

But the deeper, gnawing thing, the grief that turns life into an ocean of bitterness, belongs to the soul who has once been good, who still is good, but who has deliberately accepted some special evil into his nature and refused to let it go. Such a soul, I sincerely believe, is the most pitiable thing in all the world. Even the great sinner is less in a sense to be pitied, inasmuch as his heart is now hardened and the sense of suffering has been numbed.

Spiritual Excellence

Let us watch the process. A child, a youth, a young adult, has learned by experience what it is to dwell in the tabernacles of the Lord. He has felt the fascination of innocence. He has known what is the happy martyr-dom of being fired with the love of Jesus Christ. He has learned the secret of rejoicing in suffering, or reveling in self-sacrifice, of springing through life with that utter joy of living which belongs peculiarly to the innocent of hand and clean of heart. To such a soul, the course is quite clear. He ascends the Mount of God with unhesi-tating step. The sun of God's own love shines overhead. The way may be long, the stones may be cutting, but the truth of life is manifest, and he has no hesitation, no re-morse, no doubts, nothing but the pure delight of giv-ing, and the craving ever to give more.

One day there comes a change, and with a soul like this, the method of the change is almost invariably the same. Hitherto it has had no other comrades and com-panions than the angels of light; no others would it con-sent to know. But one day, a new angel of light appears upon the way. It may be an angel from without, in the shape of an external fascination for something appar-ently good. It may be from within, in the desire to do some good thing, to follow some particular inclination of his own, the conversion of a soul, a special good work — anything that will make him turn aside from the track along which he is drawn.

At first, all seemingly goes well. There is fruit to show for this person's labor. A soul is drawn toward God by his attention, and he tells himself that it is good to sacrifice his own perfection just a little so that another may be profited the more.

So this is the next step. The person stoops to the soul who is down. He lowers his own standard a trifle. He gives to the creature he is saving not only his proper due, not only that which, as a creature oneself, he can lawfully bestow upon another, but also a little more — that which belongs irrevocably to his own best, truest, and most loyal Friend.

But the evil does not stop there. No one ever did wrong so that good might come of it and did not sooner or later find reason to repent of his decision. Whether or not the expected good is gained is beside the mark. More often than not, the person fails to secure what he worked for, but even if he gains it, he has started a new misery that is worse. For to yield to evil is to weaken our own self, our soul, our character, our power for doing good, our peace of mind. Without God, no man can do anything. It is only in Him who strengthens us that we can do anything at all.

Hence, the one evil thing the person does leads inevitably to another. He yields "just this once, and just this far," and he finds he has taken the first step in a series of yieldings. He is not what he was; that is the first agony which torrents of tears seem unable to assuage. He is at the mercy of new forces that before had no hold upon him, and he is less able to resist them; that is the second agony, which is close akin to despair. He has taken his own course. He has separated himself from those who before had held him up. And now, in the darkness and gloom, he is hedged about by a sense of loneliness, and untruth, and helpless weakness, which makes life itself an intolerable burden.

Then comes the struggle. Humility bids him turn back while yet there is time and, since he cannot help himself, take hold of a hand that will help him. But pride whispers in his ear that this will not do, that he is his own master and must brook no interference, that he has chosen his own path and must walk along it to the bitter end. His life is now broken, he tells himself. He has lost his treasure forever, and he must carry his grief in his own heart and work out his doom as best he may.

So is the agony increased at every step, until at last the poor soul becomes partly numbed, tells himself that he has grown used to it, or soon will grow used to it, and meanwhile must submit to the inevitable. He knows he is deceiving himself. He knows the sin — if it is sin — and the agony could be removed by one bold step backward, by one humble trusting of itself to a hand that can and will support it. But these things to human nature are very hard.

Yes, they are very hard, but, thank God, not too hard. "God tempers the wind to the shorn lamb," and in all His wonderful dispositions there is nothing so wonderful as this: never was a soul left utterly alone in his misery and hopelessness who could not find succor if he would stretch out his hand and take it. And, again, God be thanked for it, many do. Pride may resist, the Devil may argue that to retreat is impossible, and human nature may pretend that the slavery is sweet. But the God of love is not beaten. In one way or another, He stretches out His hand to His beloved. A friend passes by, and at once the loneliness is gone. A word of sympathy is uttered, and the barrier of silence is broken. A prayer is poured forth, from two hearts instead of one, and the grace is given that heals the wound. All these are there, if the poor, beaten soul will take them; if he only will!

"Peter, going out, wept bitterly."[92] We are told that he wept for the remainder of his days. But surely the tears were not always bitter. Bitter tears are tears of remorse and unrepentance, of slavery to evil and inability to escape. But tears of repentance are solace to the soul and quickly grow to tears of love, and tears of love are sweet indeed. God is very good. He would not ever have any soul unhappy, not even the most stained, but He asks as the price of happiness that we should cling to Him and not stab His Heart to the quick. "Taste and see how sweet is the Lord."[93] These are the words of a penitent; and they have been found by experience to be true by millions who have "lifted up their eyes to the mountains where dwelleth light."[94]

There are many sorrows in this world, but no sorrow like that of a soul who has fallen and refuses to rise. And there are many joys, but no joy can equal the joy of the soul who may have wandered a little, but at last leaps

[92] Cf. Matt. 26:75.
[93] Ps. 33:9 (RSV = Ps. 34:8).
[94] Cf. Ps. 120:1 (RSV = Ps. 121:1).

into the arms of his Father, and clings to His neck, and tells Him he has learned his lesson, and that henceforth nothing shall tear him from His embrace. Such a soul is not worse, but far better for his bitter experience. He now knows what he did not know before. He can now help others in ways he never could have helped them otherwise. For that reason, perhaps, Peter was permitted to pass through the ordeal, and Paul and Augustine[95] and many more. The school of bitter grief has been the school of apostles, for they have learned both the evil of sin and the light and gladness and the liberating power of the love of God. "The wages of sin is death. But the grace of God, life everlasting, in Christ Jesus, our Lord."[96]

Let the truth not be forgotten: there is no merit or greatness or goodness in submitting to misery, not even because of sin. But there is much merit and strength in the happy heart that clings to God, our Lord, who has a welcome for all, but for none more than for the sheep that strayed and has returned. "Rejoice with me," He says. And if my Father is happy in my return, I will not spoil His happiness by being miserable myself.

[95] St. Augustine (354-430), Bishop of Hippo.
[96] Rom. 6:23.

Chapter Sixteen

∾

*Be courageous
in taking responsibility
for your falls*

~

If there is one thing more than another that a man most aspires to be esteemed for, it is his courage. If there is one thing more than another that a woman most admires in a man, it is his courage. If in a woman there is one thing more valued than another, it is that quiet courage which goes by many names: endurance, patience, loyalty, consistency with truth, willingness to face whatever lies before her.

Nor is there much to choose between man's courage and the courage of woman. If man has the courage of physical action, woman has the greater courage of privation. On the other hand, if man has less courage to submit to being thwarted, when woman is defeated and has to rise again, her courage tends to fail her utterly. Both have their strong points, both their limitations, but in both alike the greatest courage of all is to fight up against their weakest nature.

Spiritual Excellence

It will not be denied by many that bravery in ordinary life means the power to face and to go through hard things; cowardice in practice means the shirking of a duty. It does not matter much what excuses we may make, to what subterfuges we may resort, how successfully we may deceive ourselves or others. Let the outward show of things be what it may, the man who always takes the easiest line of life, and who always finds reasons, justifications, for taking the easiest line of life, no matter how brave, grand, and assertive those reasons may sound, is in the end no more than a coward. The modern popular affectation of a square jaw and an unbending eye, cultivated nowadays so assiduously, will not save him from self-condemnation.

On the other hand, the man who does the right thing, or, harder still, having done the wrong thing, owns up to it and makes an effort to put it right or atone for it, is a brave man, no matter what it may cost him and no matter what others may think. Indeed, the more it costs him, and the more he has public opinion to face, the braver man he must be said to be.

Now, there are various ways of facing an unpleasant and difficult situation, but three are by far the most common. One is to face it and not to look at it; to pretend that it does not exist; to put on a smile outside and hide the consciousness beneath as far as we are able; to affect bravery, all the more because we are shirkers. For instance, it is far easier, when we have done an evil deed, to deny that the deed is evil than to repent of the evil that is done; and there are very many cowards who hide themselves beneath that sham. For a person to say, "It is not wrong," when he knows very well that it is, is characteristic of a coward. Such a man, with all his show of daring, is really afraid — afraid of himself, afraid of others, afraid of the consequences of repentance. Morally such a man is of the type of those sham gentlemen whose one object in life is to make people believe they are what they are not. Such men are very common, more common than they like to think. By being at once so common and so shallow, they are easily known by those who are discerning. If they only knew how easily they were known, perhaps they would strut a little less in their garb of sham morality.

The second class is more common still, but is yet more difficult to discern. It is the class of those who, with the situation before them, make up their minds that they will live two lives. A man has done evil. The evil has entered into his life. It has become part of himself insofar as he has told himself that he can no longer do without it. He is at least braver than the first type of person, who is unwilling to acknowledge the evil he has done. At least he owns in his own heart what duty dictates, even though he tells himself that he cannot obey. The fascination holds him. To make a clean breast of it and begin again is more than he can endure. He must carry his burden in secret and put on as bold a face as he is able.

So the double life begins. Outside "whited sepulchers, but within rottenness and dead men's bones";[97] and how many there are who go to their graves smiling and esteemed, honored by men for their uprightness and courage, yet have been to themselves things of utter contempt and have dragged a weary burden behind them all their lives! One act of courage, and all might have been so different. Then there would have been no need for endless counterfeiting. Only one act of courage, following on the courage of clear understanding; and yet that one act — what an effort, for some, it implies! They prefer the burden and its consequences, no matter what the weight.

[97] Cf. Matt. 23:27.

Be courageous in taking responsibility

But there is a third class of moral coward, and this is the worst of all. The first one can despise, because he is dishonest to himself. The man who will affect to see no evil in evildoing, merely so that he may save himself the trouble of avoiding it, is his own worst enemy and may simply be set aside. The second class we pity. We long to help him. If he has not the courage to do what he ought, his weakness is, after all, one that belongs to human nature. But with the third class we are indignant, because it is the most inhuman; it is the class of those who have substituted brazenness for bravery. We all know the crew, but we do not always know its individual members, so clever are they in the art of confounding one kind of bravery with another.

A man has done wrong. He knows that to evade it, and to declare it to be no evil, is merely contemptible. He himself scorns the evildoer who adopts this device. He knows, too, that to own the wrong, and yet to fret beneath its burden, is pitiable. He has no part with those who so compel themselves to lead two lives.

Braver is it, he tells himself, if he has done wrong, to live up to it. If he has done wrong, why, then, he has done so; and wrongdoing is a sign of a man of courage. He has deeply wronged another. Such wrongdoing, he will boldly say, is but a proof of his manly vigor. He believes he must keep himself free from priest-craft and conscience. If he would enjoy life, he must defy God, man, and Devil alike. He will have none of those who have not the "courage" to sin like he, none of those chicken-hearted lovers of righteousness who will not let themselves "enjoy" life like he. "I have sinned, and what harm has befallen me?"[98] he cries with the sinner in the Scripture. And he holds up his head, and struts through life, "a law unto himself," the first principle of which is that sin is a mark of courage.

When we look at the dealings of Jesus Christ with men, it is easy to see how He singles out this third class for His most emphatic condemnation. For the merely blind He prays, "Father, forgive them, for they know not what they do,"[99] even though their blindness is chiefly from themselves. For the weak He holds out a helping hand. Even Judas, the finally impenitent traitor, He treats with pity to the end, for even Judas owned that he "had sinned."[100] But for these other cowards, who hid

[98] Ecclus. 5:4 (RSV = Sir. 5:4).
[99] Luke 23:34.
[100] Cf. Matt. 27:4.

their nature under the garb of brazenness, who sinned, and "braved" it, and taught it to others, for these He has only indignation and doom. "He who receiveth one little child in my name receiveth me. But he who shall scandalize one of these tiny children who believes in me, it were better for him that a millstone were tied about his neck and that he were cast into the depths of the sea. Woe to the world because of scandals! It must needs be that scandal should come. But woe to that man by whom the scandal cometh."[101] For the rest of men, Jesus Christ tells us, He prays. For such as these He does not pray, for He leaves them to their self-inflicted sentence.

No, if we understand aright, we shall see that this type condemns itself. For courage, as we have acknowledged at the outset of this chapter, is the power to face and go through with things that are hard. To shirk a duty, on whatever plea, is always the mark of a coward. To have done wrong and not to own it, so that we may escape the consequent repentance, is cowardice and nothing more. To have done wrong and to acknowledge it, yet to leave it unatoned for and unhealed, is cowardice of

[101]Cf. Matt. 18:5-7.

another kind, more pitiful perhaps than the first, but no less real. But to have done wrong, and to acknowledge it, and then to "brave it out" with arrogance, and mockery, and laughter; to break the law and to teach the same to others by word, and example, and compulsion: that is the greatest cowardice of all. And it meets with a coward's doom, not only in the next life, but even in this. For such a man, despite the din and recklessness around him, is devoid of friends, has killed all human sympathy, and when his day is ended, there will not be one who will feel that the world is the poorer for his loss.

Chapter Seventeen

Promote the Faith

It is a consequence of the democratic age in which we live that everything — education, government, even religion — should fall into the hands of the people. There must be teachers, but the people will decide what shall be taught. There must be legislators to frame and to pass laws, but the people must tell them what those laws shall be and see to their fulfillment. In religion, there must be priests and bishops; there must be all that inherited possession that no revolution can destroy. But the working element of the Faith, the preservation of the Faith, the spread of the Faith, the manifestation of the Faith to men — all this, from the very nature of the case, must devolve more and more upon the people. If the people do their duty, religion will be safe, go forward, and prosper, no matter what may happen. If they are wanting, no amount of preaching by its priests, or of administration by its ministers, will save it from failure.

Spiritual Excellence

Of course, in some sense, this has been always true, but it has never been truer than now, unless we except the very first ages of the Church. Then, too, she depended, perhaps more than on anything else, on the practice and example of her children. Without that, as St. Paul, St. Peter, St. James, and St. John so often hint, all preaching would be in vain. With it, apostles might be put to death, bishops and popes might be exiled and imprisoned, but for all that, the Church would conquer the world.

For that was a people's world, and the Church was a people's Church. And if the people were worthy of the Church, the world was hers. So is it in our day; the people own the world in a very real sense in this generation, and they, and almost they alone, can decide in what state the future of the Church shall be. More than prelates, more than priests and apostles and preachers, they can spread her cause or can condemn her to yet further subjection.

For this reason, it behooves us to look around and bestir ourselves. If so much lies with us, if this is one among the many consequences of our hardly earned liberty, then it behooves us to accept it and to use it well. For every gift of liberty brings with it a corresponding duty. If I am to be worthy of the one, I must look to the other.

What, then, is imposed upon me? Am I to turn missionary and preacher? Am I to become an exponent of the Church and her teaching? Am I to put religion in the first place in my life and make all the rest revolve around it? Does this entail for me the sacrifice of myself or of the things that are mine — of my family, my friends, my pleasures, my relaxations, and my interests? Or if not, what exactly is meant by, and what is the limit of, this responsibility that has come to me? For if the gaining of freedom, which is the conquest of this generation, means all this, it would seem to be only the exchanging of one kind of subjection for another.

To begin with, there are some for whom this responsibility may indeed mean all that has just been asked. Some may feel and know in their hearts that they are asked to prove their freedom, and their right use of it, by freely surrendering it — as many a rich man feels that he then makes the best use of his riches when he gives it away. Such men know beyond a doubt that nothing else but this complete surrender of themselves will satisfy them; by no other course of action will they be happy.

Spiritual Excellence

But these are by no means all. They are the very few. They are those of whom we say that they have a vocation, for a vocation in this limited and accepted sense is defined as a call to devote oneself entirely to the work of God.

Of these, then, and to these we do not here speak. We speak rather to those to whom we can say at once that the responsibility of their freedom does not exact so much.

How much, then, it will be asked, does it exact? I do not know. It will differ in each case. But in general, it may be said to be as much as an able and willing heart is able and willing to give. Circumstances are to be considered; individual characters are to be considered. A married man, with family cares and other anxieties, cannot always give as much as one who has only himself to look after; a married woman, usually even less. Again, a character that is naturally shy, and reserved, and contemplative can often make itself do less than one that is by nature open, and expansive, and active. All this must be taken into account when we make our estimates.

These things presupposed, let us now descend to something very practical. To begin with, there is one thing, and, after all, the one important thing, for the spread of the Church that every man can do: he can look to himself; he can set a good example. Conscious that wherever he goes, he carries the honor of the Church with him, he can look to it that that honor is not tarnished. Such a man will in public and before others do nothing that is unworthy of a member of the Church. Such a man will do everything that is expected of him. If he has power over others, he will do what in him lies to see that they, too, are worthy of the Church to which they belong.

By such means was Christianity mainly spread at the beginning. By such means is it spread today, although — alas, that we should have to say it — it is because of the neglect of this first duty among those who bear its name that Christianity in many places fails and falters.

But there are many who can say with the young man in the Gospel: "This I have observed from my youth. What else can I do?"[102] For these, then, let us see whether we can make any suggestions.

There are few who, if they will look around them, will not find abundant opportunities of doing good.

[102]Cf. Matt. 19:20.

Spiritual Excellence

There are our own subjects of one kind or another. These, in a quiet but unassuming way, we can influence more than we do, to think and act in the right direction. There are our own friends and equals. These, by some kind of cooperation, we can turn into towers of strength. There are the poor around us, whom we have always with us; and by "the poor" we do not merely mean those who are in need of money. We can, if we will, lend a helping hand in many places where help is needed. We can give much more than mere gold and silver. I once knew a man who made a rule for himself to spend an hour every day, if he could, in doing something for somebody, and wonderful were the devices he discovered for making himself useful.

In this lies the principle; its application may be very varied. Let us see. It is common to find men or women who offer their services to their parish priest to give instructions. Some will instruct children; some will instruct the adults who are unschooled in the Faith; some will instruct converts. Some men and women try to see to it that young people after leaving school do not fall away from the Faith. They follow them up; they see that they go to the sacraments; they support the clubs and gatherings instituted for their use.

Then there is the spreading of good literature. In many ways may this be done. There are the regular Catholic papers; there is an ever-growing output of Catholic books. If only our laymen and women would work for the circulation of these — what a world of good they would be doing!

Again, there is a kind of good work that, we have reason to fear, is very much neglected in these days. It is true we sometimes find women visiting hospitals, refuges, and even prisons; one sometimes find there Salvation Army officers; but how seldom do we find our own men! And yet why should it not be possible for them to do good work there as well as for anyone else? A man can smooth a pillow, wash a hand or a face, write a letter, lift a patient, bring a cheering book or paper — and a man can encourage a backslider to lift his face to God and determine to reform his life and begin again. And to the man who will attempt it, I can promise one thing: he will find it engrossingly interesting. He will find a new meaning in life. He will understand life as he has never understood it before — that is, from many points of view besides his own.

These, then, are some of the ways by which we can make the lay apostolate a real thing. There are many more, which a soul that is keen will not fail to discover. Only let us set to work, and something will be done. Let us work together and then, as our Lord has promised: "Where there are two or three gathered in my name, there am I in the midst of them."[103] If we want further encouragement, let us remember the words of St. James: "He who causeth a sinner to be converted from the error of his way, shall save his own soul from death, and shall cover a multitude of sins."[104] And let us remember those other words of our Lord Himself: "Come, ye blessed of my Father, possess the kingdom prepared for you from the foundation of the world. For I was hungry, and you gave me to eat. I was thirsty, and you gave me to drink. I was a stranger, and you took me in; naked, and you covered me; sick, and you visited me. I was in prison, and you came to me. . . . For, amen I say to you, as long as you did it to one of these my least brethren, you did it to me."[105]

[103]Matt. 18:20.
[104]James 5:20.
[105]Matt. 25:34-36, 40.

Appendix

~

Recommended prayers

Anima Christi

Soul of Christ, sanctify me.
Body of Christ, save me.
Blood of Christ, inebriate me.
Water from the side of Christ, wash me.
Passion of Christ, strengthen me.
O good Jesus, hear me.
Within Thy wounds, hide me.
Suffer me not to be separated from Thee.
From the malicious enemy, defend me.
In the hour of my death, call me,
and bid me come unto Thee,
that with Thy saints I may praise Thee
forever and ever. Amen.

❧

Hail, Holy Queen

Hail, Holy Queen, Mother of Mercy,
our life, our sweetness and our hope.
To thee we cry, poor banished children of Eve.
To thee do we send up our sighs,
mourning, and weeping in this valley of tears.
Turn, then, most gracious advocate,
thine eyes of mercy toward us,
and after this our exile, show unto us
the blessed Fruit of thy womb, Jesus.
O clement, O loving, O sweet Virgin Mary.
Pray for us, O holy Mother of God,
that we may be made worthy
of the promises of Christ.

❧

Hail, Mary

Hail Mary, full of grace,
the Lord is with thee.
Blessed art thou among women,
and blessed is the fruit of thy womb, Jesus.

Recommended prayers

Holy Mary, Mother of God,
pray for us sinners,
now and at the hour of our death. Amen.

∾

Our Father

Our Father,
who art in Heaven,
hallowed be Thy name.
Thy kingdom come.
Thy will be done on earth as it is in Heaven.
Give us this day our daily bread,
and forgive us our trespasses,
as we forgive those who trespass against us.
And lead us not into temptation,
but deliver us from evil. Amen.

∾

Veni, Creator Spiritus

Creator Spirit, all divine,
come visit every soul of Thine.
And fill with Thy Celestial Flame
the hearts which Thou Thyself did frame.

Spiritual Excellence

O Gift of God, Thine is the sweet,
consoling name of Paraclete.
And spring of life and fire of love,
and unction flowing from above.
The mystic sevenfold gifts are Thine,
finger of God's right hand divine,
the Father's promise sent to teach
the tongue a rich and heavenly speech.
Kindle with fire brought from above
each sense, and fill our hearts with love.
And grant our flesh, so weak and frail,
the strength of Thine which cannot fail.
Drive far away our deadly foe,
and grant us Thy true peace to know.
So we, led by Thy guidance still,
may safely pass through every ill.
To us, through Thee, the grace be shown,
to know the Father and the Son,
and Spirit of Them both, may we
forever rest our faith in Thee.
To Father and Son be praises meet,
and to the Holy Paraclete.
And may Christ send us from above,
that Holy Spirit's gift of love. Amen.

⌒

Veni, Sancte Spiritus

Come, Thou Holy Paraclete,
and from Thy celestial seat,
send Thy light and brilliancy.

Father of the poor, draw near;
Giver of all gifts, be here.
Come, the soul's true radiancy.

Come, of comforters the best,
of the soul the sweetest guest.
Come in toil refreshingly.

Thou in labor rest most sweet,
Thou art shadow from the heat,
comfort in adversity.

O Thou light, most pure and blest,
shine within the inmost breast
of Thy faithful company.

Where Thou art not, man hath naught;
every holy deed and thought
comes from Thy divinity.

Spiritual Excellence

What is soiled, make Thou pure;
what is wounded, work its cure;
what is parched, fructify.

What is rigid, gently bend;
what is frozen, warmly tend;
straighten what goes erringly.

Fill Thy faithful, who confide
in Thy power to guard and guide
with Thy sevenfold mystery.

Here Thy grace and virtue send.
Grant salvation in the end,
and in Heaven felicity. Amen. Alleluia.

___

Alban Goodier, S.J.

(1869-1939)

∾

Alban Goodier was a Jesuit who served for a time as Archbishop of Bombay, India. He was renowned for his memorable aphorisms: "A friend is the one who comes in when the whole world has gone out"; "The enthusiastic, to those who are not, are always something of a trial"; and many more.

He was also a well-respected writer who contributed many articles to the magazine *The Messenger of the Sacred Heart*. He wrote more than a dozen books, including *The Meaning of Life*, *Saints for Sinners*, *The Passion and Death of Our Lord Jesus Christ*, and *The Inner Life of the Catholic*.

Sophia Institute Press®

~

Sophia Institute® is a nonprofit institution that seeks to restore man's knowledge of eternal truth, including man's knowledge of his own nature, his relation to other persons, and his relation to God. Sophia Institute Press® serves this end in numerous ways: it publishes translations of foreign works to make them accessible for the first time to English-speaking readers; it brings out-of-print books back into print; and it publishes important new books that fulfill the ideals of Sophia Institute®.

These books afford readers a rich source of the enduring wisdom of mankind. Sophia Institute Press® makes these high-quality books available to the general public by using advanced technology and by soliciting donations to subsidize its general publishing costs. Your generosity can help Sophia Institute Press® to provide the public with editions of works containing the enduring wisdom of the ages. Please send your tax-deductible contribution to the address below. We also welcome your questions, comments, and suggestions.

For your free catalog, call:
Toll-free: 1-800-888-9344

or write:
Sophia Institute Press®
Box 5284, Manchester, NH 03108

or visit our website:
www.sophiainstitute.com